MANCHESTER

A CELEBRATION

BRIAN REDHEAD

PRINCIPAL PHOTOGRAPHY

JAN CHLEBIK

TIM HETHERINGTON

IAN LAWSON

ANDRE DEUTSCH

ACKNOWLEDGMENTS

For their invaluable help and support in the writing of this book, grateful thanks to
Pamela Bishop, Tara Johnston, Caroline Woolf and Elizabeth Jeffreys.
The recollections are mine, the collection of recent information is theirs.
Thanks also to Clare Chambers for her editing skills;
to Stuart Wilson for his outstanding design;
to Doug Jackson and Mike Cuerden for their creative input;
to Jan Chlebik, Tim Hetherington and Ian Lawson for their first class photography;
and to John Cocks for Picture Research.
Many individuals and organisations including
the Central Manchester Development Corporation, Manchester City Council,
Greater Manchester Visitor and Convention Bureau, Manchester Airport Plc
and Creative Lynx Partnership have been a source of help and encouragement,
a big thank you to them all.

ADDITIONAL PHOTOGRAPHY
COURTESY OF

Allsport, McQuillan Brown, Mr. E A Bowness, Mike Brett, BTA,
Blackpool Tourism, BT, Central Station Design, Chetham's Library, Cliff Butler, Blue Coat Press, John Cocks, Counter Image,
Crocodile Photography, David Shuttleworth, E & B Productions (Theatre) Ltd., Granada Studios Tour,
Greater Manchester Visitor & Convention Bureau, Richard Farley, Granada TV, Len Grant,
The Museum of Science & Industry in Manchester, Paul Hagert, John Hannavy, Paul Herrmann,
Dennis Hussey, Ian Howarth, Paul Jones, Lancashire Evening Post, J Leatherbarrow, Manchester Airport, Neil McAllister, Manchester Central Library,
Manchester City Art Galleries, Manchester City Council, Manchester Evening News, Manchester Museum, Mottram Hall,
Manchester University, Michael le Poer Trench, Oldham Evening Chronicle, P&G Photographics Ltd, Steve Rimmer, Rolls Royce,
Sublime Cornerhouse Exhibition, Ian Tilton, Bob Thomas, Paul Tomlin,
University of Salford, Vickers Plc, Peter Walsh, Derek Widdicombe, Stanley Willis.

MANCHESTER
A CELEBRATION

First published in Great Britain March 1993 by
André Deutsch Limited
105-106 Great Russell Street
London WC1B 3LJ

Second impression September 1993

Cataloguing-in-Publication data for this title
is available from the British Library

ISBN 0 233 98816 5

Printed in Great Britain

CONTENTS

1

PROLOGUE

History is what people make of their geography, and journalism is the first attempt at writing that history. This truth, which I am given to repeating at every opportunity, I discovered for myself in Manchester. Indeed I got my first inkling of it on my very first visit to Manchester in April 1954.

I came to the city in search of a job on the *Manchester Guardian*. I took a train from my home town, Newcastle upon Tyne, marvelled at the human habitation over the Pennines, arrived at Victoria Station and walked to Cross Street. I was early, so I stood on the opposite side of the street gazing in wonderment at the building where the great editor C.P. Scott had reigned and which the great writer Neville Cardus still adorned. Then I plucked up my courage and walked to the side-door. The commissionaire's box was empty, so I waited, wondering what to do. An elderly gentleman in a trilby and a raincoat and laden with documents came in from the street. I explained that I had come to see the editor, Mr Wadsworth.

 'Follow me,' he said. I followed him up the stairs; he pushed open an office door, entered, removed his coat and hat and signalled to me to sit down. It was indeed A. P. Wadsworth himself. He asked me about Newcastle, and I told him about its activities and its antiquities, because I had just written a series of articles for the *Newcastle Evening Chronicle*, entitled 'The Heritage of Newcastle'. (Yes, I plead guilty to being the first to use that word in that way.) Then he told

me about Manchester. I wish I had written down every word he spoke, because everything that I have learned since has demonstrated the truth of his explanation. He was not sentimental about the city, but he left me in no doubt that there was no better place in which to live and work. Then he offered me a job as a reporter. I went back home overjoyed.

'How much is he going to pay you?' my father asked. 'Do you know,' I said, 'I forgot to ask.'

I completed the academic year at Cambridge, got my degree and joined the *Manchester Guardian* on Monday 5th July 1954. In my first three weeks, as part of my work, I went to two plays and to three concerts, to a cotton mill and to the cotton exchange, to three schools and to two colleges, to a dockers' meeting and to a Town Hall banquet. I saw Cyril Washbrook in the street and then opening the batting at Old Trafford cricket ground. I saw John Barbirolli in the bar at the Midland Hotel and then conducting the Hallé Orchestra at the Free Trade Hall. I saw paintings by L.S. Lowry and then I saw Mr Lowry himself.

At the end of those three weeks a college friend rang me to ask if I was enjoying myself in Manchester. I enthused.

'Manchester,' I said, somewhat grandly, 'is big enough for things to happen, but small enough to attend them and to attend upon them.' That was true then, and it is true now. And that is why Manchester is a city to celebrate.

Manchester a Celebration

Opposite: (1) On the streets of modern Manchester: the new Metrolink transport system is symbolic of the city's history of innovation.

" Manchester is the only English city which can look London in the face, not merely as a regional capital but as a rival version of how men should live in a community. "

AJP Taylor

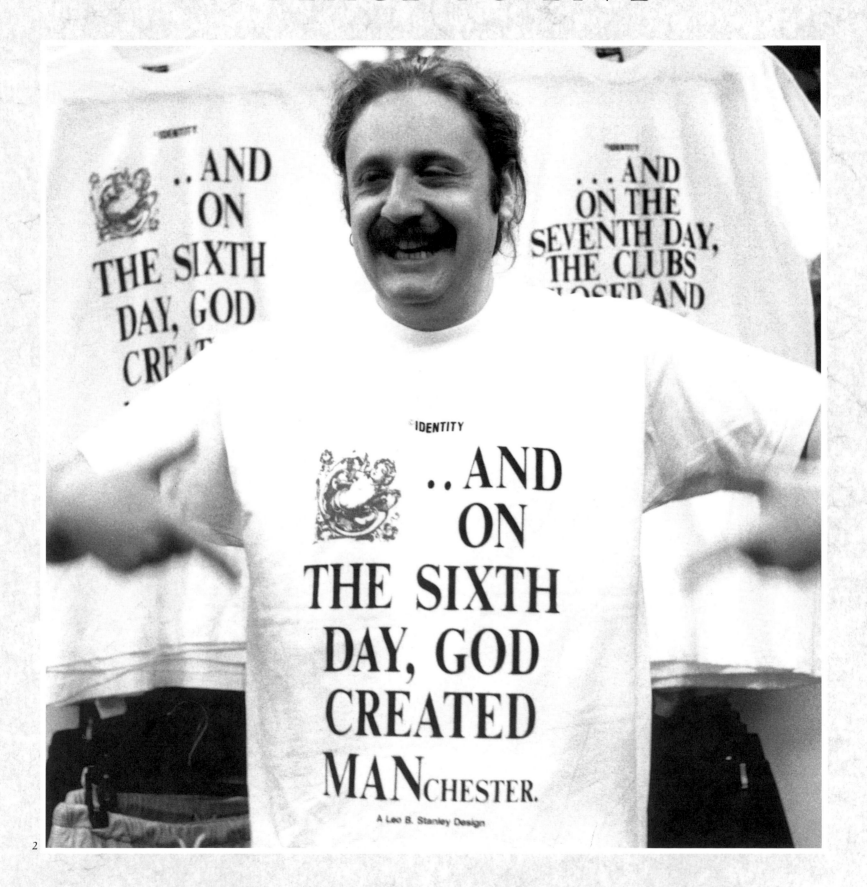

To understand Manchester, it is necessary to know both where it is – its geography – and what goes on there, its history.

Manchester, situated on the west side of the Pennine hills, is the capital, in every sense, of the North West of England, where the modern world was born. It was here that people first took to industry, and industry to them, giving them a head start which they have never surrendered. The first rush of inhabitants came from the Pennines to follow their fortunes downstream towards the steam age. Their enterprise and their merchant skills were both the foundation of Britain's wealth and the centre of the world economy. All the characteristics of those industrial and commercial beginnings – the acumen, the initiative, the invention – are now the inspiration for the present. Today, seven million people live in the North West, and they manufacture almost half of Britain's goods.

The North West was not only the birthplace of the first Industrial Revolution, it is the birthplace of the second. The first stored programme computer in the world was built at Manchester University by Freddie Williams and Tom Kilburn. The world's first commercially available computer was built at Ferranti's just up the road. And there is no better illustration of the old truth that what Manchester thinks today, London thinks tomorrow, and the world the day after, than this: when Vincent de Ferranti invited the President of the Board of Trade in London to contribute government money to the development costs of that first commercial computer, the President, Stafford Cripps, replied: 'It is the Government's considered opinion that there will never be a need in Britain for more than two computers.'

Manchester knew better. Whatever business you mention, the chances are that in and around Manchester they did it first and they do it best.

Part of Manchester's commercial success must be put down to its excellent transport and communication links. It has the best motorway network in Europe, making not only everywhere within the region easily accessible, but the rest of Britain and Europe too. But then this area had the first motorway in Britain, the first scheduled air service, the first passenger train service, the first industrial canal, and today boasts the first light-rail Metrolink system which runs on both rail and road tracks. In every age of transport, this is where it all began.

All this innovation should not surprise us from a city famous as a seat of learning. It was here that the father of modern chemistry, John Dalton, taught the father of modern physics, James Joule, and their successors now adorn one of the biggest university precincts in Europe. The applied research here is of direct benefit to industry; research and development for the common good. And those with potential are nurtured from a young age: Manchester has the best day school for boys in the land, Manchester Grammar School, where entry is by fierce competition, and the finest school in Europe for the musically gifted – Chetham's Hospital, where entry is simply by audition.

Manchester is not just a place of work, however. It is a place for leisure; music, sport and the arts. The Hallé Orchestra was the first fulltime orchestra in Britain, the first where the same performers who attended the rehearsal turned up for the performance – a courtesy still not always observed in London. Manchester had the first repertory theatre in the world and is given to opening theatres rather than closing them. It is rich in radio, its television is broadcast to millions worldwide and its very own *Guardian* became a newspaper of national and international renown.

The sportsmen and women of the North West have the same missionary zeal. Manchester United is the most famous football club in the world. The region has the best supported football teams in Britain and yet more boys play football here on Saturdays even than watch it. And the Old Trafford cricket ground in Manchester holds the record for the largest attendance at a County Match on a single day. The biggest municipal park in Britain is Heaton Park in Manchester, and it is claimed that the largest golf course in the country is the Manchester Golf Club at Middleton.

The North West may have invented work, but it also invented paid holidays, organising the first annual holidays at the seaside for working people – Wakes Weeks. A good standard of living has always been important here: when factory workers elsewhere were still the unhappy tenants of grasping landlords, Lancashire mill workers owned their own homes.

Today their successors treasure their homes and surroundings – the Pennines, where it all began, are rarely out of sight and never out of mind. They are more than monuments of natural beauty; they are the permanence of this part of the United Kingdom. The people know their geography is without equal. Their history is their response to it. And they are happy for others to share in their good fortune. Come and join us, they say, and see for yourselves that there is no better place to live a full life.

4

5

6

Pages 12/13: (3) By night as by day, the city hums with energy.

Informality is our style, (4) whether it is young people relaxing in the continental atmosphere of a pavement cafe; (5) police preparing for duty during the visit of the Pope; (6) a St John Ambulance volunteer providing helpful directions, (7) or a traffic warden enjoying the sunshine. (8) And there are always our spacious squares in which to meet and talk.

8

7

15

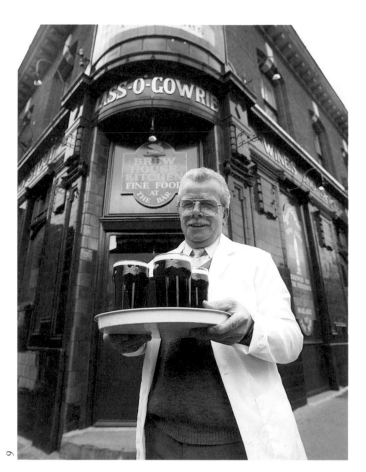

(9, 10, 11, 12, 13) *The English pub might have been invented to explain the word 'Welcome'. It is where we meet old friends and make new ones, where we eat, drink, debate and celebrate. Nowhere is the tradition of hospitality in better hands than in Manchester, the home of good beer.*

11

12

13

Pages 18/19: Countryside is always close at hand: (14) comfortable family homes nestle among the woodland twenty minutes' drive from the city centre.

For a compact region, we enjoy a rich diversity of settings. (15, 16, 17, 18, 19) Businessmen and women stroll through the elegant cloisters of Manchester's Town Hall; fruit and flower sellers add colour to our streets; village shops like the local post office in the village of Delph are lasting institutions and families enjoy the serenity of country living in former mill towns like Uppermill.

17

18

21

22

23

(20) Only six cities in the world outside Italy rate as fashion centres worthy of an Emporio Armani. Manchester is, naturally, one of them. (21) Alongside Emporio Armani is the pedestrianised shopping area of the city centre. (22) Young designers make their debut in the 150 shops of Affleck's Palace, a wonderland of youth and style. (23) By contrast, our young people still have a place in their hearts for tradition among the stylish modern shops of St Ann's Square.

24

25

(24, 25) There is a place in the sun for everyone in Manchester.

AN HISTORIC PLACE

One Friday evening in September 1978 on the BBC television programme *Homeground*, which was broadcast from Manchester, I asked the studio audience what they thought was the most historic part of the North West of England. Was it Chester, with its soaring Roman walls, its 900-year-old cathedral, and its famous 'Rows', those elegant covered arcades dating from the Middle Ages? Was it Lancaster, where the Old Pretender tried to regain the crown of England lost by his father? The Old Pretender called himself James III at Lancaster in 1715, but nobody took much notice. Or would they alight on Castlefield, I asked, confident that the bulk of the audience was thinking, where?

It is true, I said, that not much of the castle remains, and even less of the field, but nonetheless a very good case can be made to support the claim that Castlefield is the most historic spot in the North West. And then, egged on by Barri Jones, Professor of Archaeology at Manchester University, I explained that Castlefield is the place in Manchester where the River Irwell and the River Medlock meet. And it is historic because it is a very lived-on piece of land, with layer upon layer of history going back two thousand years.

That was in 1978, when Castlefield was a site of dereliction and decay. Few people knew about it, and those who did tried to pretend it wasn't there. Today a lot of people know about this fascinating and historic area, and more are discovering it all the time. It is a joy to see, and my first call when I wish to introduce a visitor to Manchester.

When it was meadowland it was the place where the Romans built a great fort in Manchester. Later it became the place where the first major canal in Britain was cut and where the first passenger railway station in the world was built.

It was there that the proud men of the eighteenth century built themselves fine houses and then allowed many of them to be pulled down to make way for the nineteenth century.

It was there that the cotton merchants of Manchester built the monuments to their commercial skill.

Barri Jones and his colleagues had discovered that in Roman times Castlefield was not only a fort but a port, and that port developed along the banks of the Irwell. We know for certain that by 1741 the port had a new quay, at the foot of what is now Quay Street. But it was the building of the Bridgewater Canal by the first Duke of Bridgewater which made Castlefield a great water junction.

Its purpose was to carry coal from the Duke's mines at Worsley to Manchester's new factories. He also sold the coal to local people at fourpence a hundredweight (about fifty kilos).

In 1764 the Canal reached Castlefield and extensive wharfs and warehouses were built there, along with a large number of houses for the growing population. Forty years later the Rochdale Canal was built and it joined the Bridgewater at Castlefield, making Castlefield the spaghetti junction of the canal system.

The great waterways system stretching out from the Castlefield basin was no sooner in business than men began to toy with plans for railway systems. By then Manchester was trading with the world, particularly in cotton, and canals alone could not cope with the flow of goods. The first plan for a railway between Manchester and Liverpool was proposed in 1822. That came to nothing, but a second succeeded. And before long the last of the Roman fort vanished beneath huge Victorian railway viaducts, and most of the houses gave way to railway sheds and other buildings. Then the railways themselves moved on, and Castlefield started a long decline into oblivion that could have been fatal.

When I argued on television in 1978 that Castlefield was the most interesting place in the North West and we ought to do something about it, nobody at first seemed to want to know. But forces were already at work and the following year it was designated a conservation area. Today it is Britain's first Urban Heritage Park. And rightly so.

It is a magnificent monument to the past, but more than that, it is a place where far-sighted people are now preserving and re-using the best of the past. The venerable buildings are being used to create new places for living, working and leisure. The old Liverpool Road Station complex, the first passenger railway buildings in the world, now houses the Museum of Science and Industry, which is well worth visiting. And there is also the museum's Air and Space Gallery in the former Lower Campfield Market, which is a magnificent iron and glass structure.

The sprawling Castlefield basin and the Bridgewater and Rochdale Canals have been restored by the Central Manchester Development Corporation. The waters are busy with barges once more, carrying not coal but people. You can walk along restored towpaths right through the heart of the city, something that hasn't been possible for years.

Run-down canal warehouses have been rescued from dereliction and turned into elegant new homes or attractive offices. A Victorian church is a new recording studio, a run-down stable block is a brand new pub, and a lock-keeper's cottage is the prettiest office in Manchester. Round the corner, Granada Television has given its own unique touch to several old railway and canal warehouses, turning them into Granada Studios Tour, the only television theme park in Europe.

In fact there is so much going on in Castlefield, and so many people coming to see it, that a new management company has been set up just to look after the area. It is run by Britain's very first 'urban rangers', who patrol the heritage park to look after visitors. It is all part of the charm of Castlefield, an enduring symbol of Manchester's past, present and future.

Page 25: (26) Narrowboats ply the canal at Castlefield, right in the heart of the city.

27

(27) First came the Romans, commemorated in a mural at the site of their Castlefield fort. (28) Cobbles, carts and ancient mills styled our life in the nineteenth century. (29) Artists and designers have revived the mellow Old Schoolhouse at Castlefield. (30) Pleasure craft, successors to the working boats of old, moor in the sunshine beneath a vintage railway arch that today carries the new Metrolink system.

28

31

32

33

34

35

(32, 33) We discover ourselves through our heritage: in the Museum of Science and Industry in Castlefield, as a small boy in rapt fascination of a refurbished railway engine or through the glories of early aircraft built in the region.
(35) Today, Castlefield lends itself to civilised modern living: (34) in the friendship of the morning sun along revitalised canal towpaths; (31) in the creation of a New York street at Granada Studios Tour, Europe's only TV theme park, (36) or mingling in the cosmopolitan atmosphere of carnival day.

36

37

38

(37, 38) Where once they carried coal and cotton, today the canals thrive with craft for leisure and living.

Captain Ivan Smirnoff, the famous Russian pilot, looked down on Manchester Airport and he did not like what he saw.

'It will not do,' he said. 'It is too small.' And he flew his KLM airliner on to Liverpool.

Manchester's city fathers were appalled. They had been pinning their hopes on Barton Airport, alongside the Manchester Ship Canal and the great industrial estate of Trafford Park, and now they were being spurned by one of the leading airlines of Europe.

The year was 1934, and five years earlier Manchester had become Britain's first municipality to be licensed to run an aerodrome. They had their heads in the clouds. Captain Smirnoff brought them down to earth with a bump. But they took the hint and their search for a better site eventually took them to a large field in a place called Ringway.

This is the stuff legends are made of – but they have been creating legends like this in Manchester for a very long time.

As I drive along the motorways that weave around the city, travel by express train to London, or take off from the fastest-growing airport in Europe, I often reflect that Manchester is enjoying the fruits of a long love affair with transport.

After all, this is the city where Mr Rolls met Mr Royce and where Mr Ford set up shop in Britain. This is where they dug the first proper canals, ran the first 'bus' service, opened the first municipal airport in the country and the first passenger railway station in the world.

It all started with the Romans of course. They built roads in Manchester as they did everywhere else, but when they went home the Britons they left behind seemed to lose the habit of moving about for several hundred years.

The switch from farming to industry set it all going again, but with the roads that existed, shifting raw materials and finished goods was no easy matter. Packhorse trails and turnpike roads fanned out from Manchester, but they were not very good.

So they ditched the roads and took to the water. In 1736 there was a scheme to use the Mersey and the Irwell, but the rivers round here are not easily navigable and it was never more than a stopgap measure, a tinkering with the problem. Something entirely new was needed.

It was left to the third Duke of Bridgewater to solve Manchester's problem by building the Bridgewater Canal in 1760.

Within a few years, canals had spread across the country. But they still had serious limitations, as barge travel was agonisingly slow. The railway age came none too soon.

When local businessmen were discussing a rail-link between Manchester and Liverpool in 1822, they modestly called it their 'Grand British Experimental Railway'.

Four years later, in 1826, with help from engineer George Stephenson, the Liverpool & Manchester Rail-Road Company got a bill through Parliament and set about building a pioneering railway line.

Even when the thirty-one mile line had been built, through tunnels and across bridges and viaducts up to sixty feet high, they were still undecided about whether to use steam or horsepower on the line. In an inspired public relations exercise, the company offered £500 for the best locomotive. The result was one of the greatest railway events of all time – the Rainhill Trials of October 1829.

Five engines entered, fifteen thousand people turned out to watch, and Stephenson's 'Rocket' chugged to victory. The stage was set for the Grand Opening on the 15th September 1830.

Everybody who was anybody was aboard the eight inaugural trains that left Liverpool that day – 722 VIPs in thirty coaches, with the Duke of Wellington, then Prime Minister, as guest of honour. But at Rainhill, where they stopped for water, triumph turned to tragedy. William Huskisson, MP for Liverpool and President of the Board of Trade, stepped down from his carriage to chat to the Duke – and was run over and crushed by the 'Rocket'. He died the same evening, and it was a gloomy party who returned to Liverpool later that day. Nonetheless the railway was open.

In its first full year the Liverpool & Manchester carried nearly half a million passengers, and by 1835 was shifting nearly 350,000 tons of freight a year, a third of it coal. Before long, nine separate railway companies had converged on the city.

The first London Road Station (now Piccadilly) opened in 1842, and two years later the L&M steamed across the city to the new Victoria Station. By 1900 this was one of the biggest in the country and it is still mightily impressive, with its 160 yard Edwardian facade.

The last great city station was Central, with its soaring iron and glass roof, 210 feet wide in a single span, which the Midland Railway opened in 1880. It closed in 1969 and, as an example of Manchester's policy of recycling its great buildings, the huge arch now looks down on the Greater Manchester Exhibition and Event Centre, which puts on everything from pop to Pavarotti.

It was the Midland Railway who built Manchester's most famous hotel, the Midland (now called the Holiday Inn Crowne Plaza Midland!), across the road from Central Station. On one much recited occasion the pianist, Mark Hamburg, who had been playing with the Hallé Orchestra, could not get to sleep for the noise of the trains in the station. Finally in exasperation he summoned the manager to his room. 'Tell me, my good man,' he said, 'when does this hotel get to Euston?'

And it was at the Midland Hotel in 1904, that the Hon. Charles Rolls persuaded Mr Henry Royce to give him sole rights to sell motor cars produced at the Royce works in Hulme. Within months the firm was producing the 40hp Silver Ghost which brought them world renown.

These makers of superior motor cars doubtless looked askance at the antics of an upstart American company that came roaring into Manchester a few years later. Henry Ford had arrived. On 23 October 1911 the first British-built Ford car, a Model T, rolled off the primitive assembly line. It was the first of three hundred thousand Model Ts made in Manchester.

But public transport was already competing with the motor car. People had been moving out to the new 'garden suburbs' and needed to get to and from work. By the turn of the century Manchester was girdled with a vast electric tramway network.

As most people lived within a mile or two of their nearest station, suburban trains caught on. Lines were electrified to increase capacity — as early as 1916 on the Bury route, and 1931 on the Altrincham line. The stage was set even then for the Metrolink supertrams.

Bus services also expanded and, in the face of mounting costs and rising car ownership, local corporations amalgamated in 1974 to form Greater Manchester Transport. Within two years it had the biggest bus fleet outside London. Now several of these commuter strands have come together to create another first for Manchester — Metrolink. These smooth and sophisticated supertrams are as different from the old bone-shakers as Concorde is from a Dakota, and they glide along railway lines and city streets with equal facility.

And over at Manchester Airport (which they stopped calling Ringway years ago) they've been expanding at the rate of £1 million a week. They confidently expect to soar into the world's top ten airports by the dawn of the twenty-first century, handling thirty million passengers a year. Helping the airport to cope with all this growth is the new Terminal 2 complex. In 1992 this was one of the UK's largest single construction projects, with a site area totalling over one million square metres — equal to two hundred soccer pitches.

Captain Ivan Smirnoff would have smirked.

Manchester a Celebration

Page 33: (39) Metrolink, the most modern on-street transport system in Europe, quietly whisks commuters and shoppers through St Peter's Square in the city centre and out to the suburbs.

40

41

Manchester's inventive nature finds imaginative roles for its grand old buildings. (40, 41) Central Station, once almost derelict, is thriving again as the G-Mex Centre, a colossal exhibition and convention hall. (42) From modernised Piccadilly Station, hourly first-class trains bring London within two-and-a-half hours' travel. (43, 44) Victoria Station, with its magnificent façade, is now a hub for the Metrolink system.

45

47

Travelling to and from Manchester has never been easier. Each year 12 million passengers already use the airport, which also handles 73,300 tonnes of cargo (45). The panorama (46) shows the development (extreme left) of the new terminal, opening in 1993, which will increase passenger capacity to 24 million a year. (47) A stylishly-designed rail link will carry visitors and business people to the city centre in 15 minutes. (48) Air traffic controllers handle 94 airlines with 170 destinations worldwide. (49) And we boast our own fleet of distinctive aircraft in the British Airways livery.

46

48

49

(52, 53) We built the first motorway in Britain here in the North West. Today, with a quarter of the country's motorways, we have the best network in Britain. (50) Cyclists find time to relax in the sun. We also provide them with special cycle lanes on city streets. (51) Commuters and visitors view the city from a new angle by using the water bus which glides past Exchange Quay into the Manchester Ship Canal.

50

51

52

3

(54, 55) And as the sun sinks slowly in the West, travel assumes a timeless quality.

Manchester has always had plenty to say on the subject of governing its people, but before it could tell the nation what to think, it had to have some recognised spokesmen.

When sixty thousand working people, dressed in their Sunday best, gathered in St Peter's Fields in the middle of Manchester on 16 August 1819, they were there to hear the case for the reform of Parliament from the radical Henry Hunt MP.

Hunt was arrested, and when the Hussars drew their sabres and rode into that orderly crowd, there were no Manchester Members of Parliament present to protest at the killings. There were none because Manchester *had* none. In spite of the huge expansion of Manchester, Liverpool and all the cotton towns, Lancashire had the same number of MPs in Westminster – fourteen – in 1819 as it had in 1519.

But this one event, known as the Peterloo Massacre, changed all that. The horror it provoked accelerated the cause of parliamentary democracy and, in the subsequent Great Reform Bill of 1832, some at least of the anomalies and injustices were removed: the region at last had representation.

It is, I think, fair to argue that the impetus for that small but crucial change in the democratic system came from Manchester. And it went on pushing to win more seats in Parliament and to give more men, and eventually all men, the vote. It was a signal to the world.

The system of representation, begun only thirteen years after Peterloo, has been modified continuously since, and now both men and women of Manchester elect a total of ninety-nine city councillors, nine MPs, and two Members of the European Parliament.

Manchester was responsible for many political reforms. It was the home of probably the most successful political lobby in the history of this country.

The Corn Laws of 1815 had forbidden the import of foreign corn until home-grown corn had reached the famine price of £4 a quarter, ten shillings (50p) a bushel. This was fine if you were a rich farmer, but hell if you were a poor mill worker. Dear bread and low wages are a recipe for misery. Mill owners campaigning against the Corn Laws argued that it made more sense to buy Europe's surplus corn with increased cotton exports, because in that way employment would be guaranteed in the mills and bread would be cheap. In short, what they sought was not restraint on trade, but Free Trade.

Pause for a roll of drums.

In September 1838, a small group of cotton merchants met in the York Hotel in King Street, Manchester, to found the Anti-Corn Law League. The League's vigorous campaign attracted such support that in January 1840 a wooden hall was erected in Peter Street to accommodate their audiences. It was built in less than a fortnight – a fine illustration of the industry of the Manchester workforce – and was called the Free Trade Hall.

Two men dominated the Anti-Corn Law League: Richard Cobden, a calico manufacturer in Manchester, and John Bright, a Rochdale mill owner. Along with George Wilson they formed what Disraeli called 'the Manchester School'.

Both Cobden and Bright got themselves elected to Parliament and were instrumental in persuading the Prime Minister, Robert Peel, to repeal the hated laws.

Peel's action split the Conservative Party and ruined his own political career, but the League members were ecstatic. Manchester declared a public holiday, and masters and men alike paraded joyfully through the streets. To this day the Free Trade Hall in Peter Street, now rebuilt in stone and home to the Hallé Orchestra, stands as a monument to that political achievement.

But Manchester's dominance of the political life of the country did not end with Free Trade. The Trades Union Congress was born in Manchester, in the Mechanics' Institute on Princess Street.

Two Manchester printing workers, Samuel Caldwell Nicholson and William Henry Wood, respectively President and Secretary of the Manchester and Salford Trades Council, called a meeting in June 1868 at the Mechanics' Institute for a 'Congress of the representatives of the Trades Councils and other similar federations of trade societies'. Thirty-four men representing 118,000 members attended. And a similar conference has been held every year since. In 1968 it fell to a Lancashire weaver, George Woodcock, General Secretary of the TUC, to unveil the commemorative plaque at 103 Princess Street, which now houses the Museum of Labour History.

It was in Manchester too that the fight for women's suffrage began. Among the founders of the Manchester Women's movement were Emmeline Pankhurst and her daughters.

In the summer of 1903, one of the daughters, Sylvia, was asked by the Independent Labour Party to paint a hall at Hightown, Salford, in memory of her father, a local lawyer and political campaigner. She and her mother were horrified to learn that women would not be allowed to attend meetings in that very hall. So Emmeline invited a group of her friends to her house on 10 October 1903, and the Women's Social and Political Union (WSPU), whose members became known as suffragettes, was born.

Two years later Emmeline's eldest daughter, Christabel, a law graduate from Manchester University, went to a Liberal election meeting with her friend Annie Kenney. The meeting was in the Free Trade Hall, and the two girls asked whether the incoming Liberal government would give women the vote. They were thrown out of the meeting, unanswered, and when they continued to protest outside, they were arrested and sent to Strangeways Prison. Their refusal to pay the fine imposed ensured the WSPU nationwide publicity. And the battle was on.

All that is splendidly commemorated at the Pankhurst Centre in the family's old house at 62 Nelson Street, Manchester. Commemorated, I might add, by continued campaigning for equality, not just by proud recollection.

People's rights – or the lack of them – were certainly dear to the heart of another woman whose work did much to correct social injustices in the middle of the nineteenth century. Social worker, prison visitor and novelist Elizabeth Gaskell was arguably the most famous woman in Manchester at this time, and many critics think her industrial novels, *Mary Barton* and *North and South*, reflect the conditions of the working classes more accurately even than the work of another famous Manchester dweller, Friedrich Engels.

While in Manchester Engels regularly attended Hallé concerts and often wrote for the *Manchester Guardian*. I can only applaud his good taste on both counts.

During the same period, Engels met Mary Burns, an Irish working class girl with whom he lived until her death, and it was through Mary and her sister, Lizzie, that Engels learned about working class life in the city.

By 1844 he had enough material to write *The Condition of the Working Class in England*.

Manchester can justly claim to be a city of conscience. It was a Welfare City long before there was a Welfare State, a city where the poor or the dispossessed were not overlooked.

I remember, at the very first civic banquet I attended at the Town Hall way back in 1954, an old alderman patiently explaining to me that Manchester was not only a fine city in which to be gainfully employed, but also a good city in which to be poor.

'If such misfortune were to befall you,' he said, 'you would still be better off here than anywhere else.' And he meant it, generously.

Manchester
a Celebration

Page 43: (56) Manchester led the world's development and the battle for democracy. A cartoon of that period records the tragic but historic Peterloo Massacre.

57

58

Manchester prides itself on being first. (58) Inventions and scientific discoveries which changed the world are emblazoned on posters in the city. (57) A distinctive blue heritage plaque commemorates the site of the gathering which helped to enfranchise British men. (59) More than fifty years later, Emmeline Pankhurst and her daughter Christabel founded the movement for women's suffrage and suffered imprisonment before votes for women, too, were achieved. (60) Today the Free Trade Hall, magnificently rebuilt from the original wooden structure, houses the city's famous Hallé Orchestra.

59

(61, 62) *The banners of the Tin Plate Workers Society, the oldest banner of its kind in the world, dating from 1821, and of the Co-operative Women's Guild now grace the Museum of Labour History in Princess Street.*

63

One person only – if we exclude St Peter and St Ann, Queen Victoria and Prince Albert – one citizen of Manchester alone has both a street in the city centre named after him and a statue erected to him. The street is on the corner of Albert Square; the statue is in the entrance to the Town Hall, and the man is John Dalton, the father of modern chemistry.

John Dalton came to Manchester in 1793 to teach, and by the time he died in 1844 he was so famous that his body lay in state in the Town Hall and one hundred coaches followed his funeral cortège to Ardwick cemetery. It was his research into the behaviour of clouds which laid the foundations of meteorology as a science, but he is best remembered for his atomic theory.

In Manchester Town Hall there is also a statue of Dalton's most famous pupil, James Prescott Joule – forever remembered for giving his name to a unit of energy. Joule said that Dalton 'possessed a rare power of engaging the affection of his pupils for scientific truth'.

And it was in Manchester that Rutherford, who was to split the atom, an act which would have delighted Dalton, uttered his most famous remark:

'There is only physics; everything else is stamp collecting.'

Manchester itself seems to have a rare power for attracting those who wish to learn – its higher education establishments, including no fewer than four universities, offer a vast range of courses to students from all over the world.

The University of Manchester Institute of Science and Technology has many collaborative projects with industry, and was the first institution of its kind to win the Queen's Award for Export. 'Not for exporting us,' said one student wag when the award was announced. 'A fifth of us come from overseas.' Though in truth both its students and discoveries are welcome the world over.

Manchester University, founded in 1851, had its origins in Owens College which began as a house in Quay Street for sixty-two students. It developed into the Victoria University of Manchester, whose purpose was to bring the new world of science and technology into the old world of liberal education. Today it has an international reputation. Applications to the universities and the former polytechnic – now the Manchester Metropolitan University – have soared as sixth-formers throughout Britain see Manchester increasingly as the country's youth-culture capital.

Manchester Business School and the Royal Northern College of Music enjoy an international reputation for excellence in their specific fields. Other higher education institutes include Manchester College of Arts and Technology and the South Manchester College. An important part of all their various curricula is the chance to live in one of the most stimulating cities in which to learn.

All these educational establishments are expanding and advancing. University College, Salford, for example, started a Performing Arts and Media Studies course and in one year alone its best pop group won the John Lennon Award, its best jazz pianist a Dave Brubeck scholarship to Berkeley, California, and a radio student a medal at the New York Radio Festival.

And if that is not radical enough, at the new Manchester Institute for Popular Culture, students can take a master's degree in such areas as football, house music, fanzines and nightclubs.

But academia is only one part of student life in Manchester. The city offers so much in the way of entertainment – restaurants, bars, cinemas, sports clubs and nightclubs – that it is a miracle undergraduates ever get any work done. Many popular haunts can be found along Whitworth Street, among them the *avant garde* cinema, bar and art gallery called 'Cornerhouse', and the internationally renowned Haçienda. It is not surprising that students, whatever their subject, arts or sciences, medicine or music, flock to Manchester. It is simply a great place to be young.

It should not be imagined that the non-student population of Manchester is disadvantaged when it comes to educational facilities: Manchester is a city of readers, having had municipal public libraries since 1852 and a free public library longer than any city in Europe.

It was the gift of Humphrey Chetham. He was a rich merchant and banker and when he died in 1651 he left most of his fortune to found a school for boys, Chetham's Hospital School, and alongside it a free library. Together they are still a beautiful, unspoiled seventeenth century enclave. And the library is a miracle of preservation; the furniture and fittings are much the same as they were when it was first equipped in 1654. (Friedrich Engels, incidentally, did his homework here when he was researching *The Condition of the Working Class in England*.)

Everyone who knows Manchester knows the Central Library, if only from the outside. Described by the historian A.J.P. Taylor as a wedding cake on a gigantic scale, it stands in St Peter's Square and was opened by King George V in 1934. Beehive might be a better description not only of its rotundity, but of its activity. I remember inquiring one day in 1971 of the then Chief Librarian how many people used the library every day.

'Four thousand,' he replied. 'And they borrow four million books every year.'

Today, the Central Library provides excellent facilities for disabled readers. In 1982 the library became the first in Europe to buy a Kurzweil Reading Machine, a talking book service for the blind and visually impaired. The machine is able to scan pages and read them aloud, providing the pleasure of reading to those for whom the printed word would otherwise be inaccessible.

Manchester not only has all this, but also the prettiest subscription library in the land – the Portico Library – which opened in 1806. Its first secretary was Dr Peter Mark Roget, the same Roget who was to compile the famous *Thesaurus of English Words and Phrases*. Manchester also boasts the greatest private library in England, the John Rylands Library on Deansgate. It is one of the finest Victorian Gothic buildings in Britain, housing some of the greatest books and manuscripts in the world.

John Rylands was a Manchester merchant, rich and successful. He lived in Longford Hall and had a fine private library there. He died in 1888, at the age of eighty-seven, leaving a huge fortune with which his third wife, Enriqueta Augustina, decided to build a library in the middle of Manchester. It was to be a fitting tribute to her husband.

She commissioned a young architect, Basil Champneys, and he set to work with the very best masons, sculptors, metal-workers, carpenters and wood carvers that could be found. The result is incomparable. The John Rylands Library was ten years in the building and worth every minute of it. It is not only a magnificent building, it houses two superb collections – one of books and one of manuscripts, which Mrs Rylands purchased for half a million pounds. Because it was a private library there was, about twenty years ago, some fear for its future, but that future was secured when it became part of the Library of Manchester University. Indeed the University has adopted its title and the University Library is now called the John Rylands University Library of Manchester.

With the quality and variety of its libraries and educational institutions, available both to the local community and students from all over the world, Manchester's reputation as a city of learning is assured.

Manchester a Celebration

Education is for enjoying: (64) musing over Old Masters in one of our twenty-three art galleries; (68) preparing to be prodigies at Chetham's School of Music; (66, 67) the excitement of discovery or the concentration of creativity.
(65) Meanwhile, back in the playground, boys will be boys.

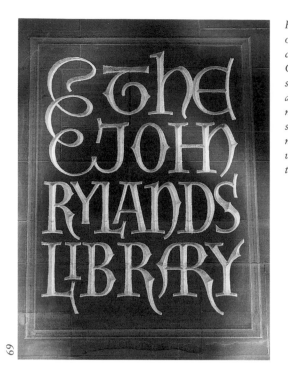

69

Fortune favours the city: (69, 70) the wife of a wealthy merchant, John Rylands, commissioned the young architect Basil Champneys, with the best masons, sculptors and carvers to be found, to build a magnificent library on Deansgate in his memory. Then she spent £500,000 on superb collections of books and manuscripts. (71, 72) Students of the visual arts express themselves in traditional and avant-garde forms.

70

71

72

73

74

56

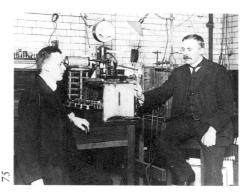

(73, 74) *Happiness is a university degree!*
(75) *Ernest Rutherford (photographed here with Hans Geiger) first split the atom in the University of Manchester.*
(77) *Now we have four universities and 45,000 students from 120 nations on the biggest campus in Europe which includes Britain's largest medical school.*
(76) *Today, we also lead the world in high-tech research.*

(78) The University of Salford, whose students challenge neighbouring Manchester to Britain's other University Boat Race, established the National Robotics Centre, a unique unit linking academic excellence with industry.
(79) And across the city, the classic floodlit lines of the Congregational College in Whalley Range which now hosts major conferences.

78

79

The arts are the emblem of civilisation and music is the greatest of all the arts because the form and the content are indistinguishable. I forget which *Guardian* critic it was who said that. From the moment I began working in Manchester I was overjoyed at the richness of the musical life. It not only had the Hallé Orchestra, but the BBC Northern (now the BBC Philharmonic), the Chamber Music Society, the Mid-day Concerts, and even Louis Armstrong at Belle Vue. A marvellous addition has been the Manchester Camarata — the busiest freelance orchestra outside London.

But Manchester is a city where music is not only performed, but studied. The first piano recital I covered for the *Guardian* was given by a sixth-former at Manchester Grammar School called John Ogdon — who went on to be the first British winner of the Tchaikovsky Competition in Moscow.

In his last will and testament Humphrey Chetham, a rich merchant and banker, said that he was leaving his money to found a Bluecoat School for 'the sons of honest, industrious and painful parents, and not of wandering or idle beggars or rogues'. Chets, as the pupils say, not Cheats.

Chetham's was a boys' school for three hundred years, but in 1969 it became Chetham's Hospital School of Music, a co-educational school for the musically gifted. It is not easy to get into; daddy can have all the money in the world, but it will make no difference. There is no academic entrance examination, no intelligence test. There is simply an audition. You do not have to be an infant prodigy to get in, but you have to have within you the ability to make music. And there is nowhere else to match it.

And when the Royal Manchester College of Music merged with the Northern School of Music to form the Royal Northern College of Music, it moved in 1973 into the first purpose-built conservatoire in Britain since the nineteenth century. It now provides the country with a stream of excellent performers.

The city was also rich in composers learning their trade — Peter Maxwell Davies, Harrison Birtwhistle, Sandy Goehr, John McCabe. I remember sitting in the Free Trade Hall next to John's mother when the Hallé gave the first performance of his *Chagall's Windows*, and I shared in her delight.

In 1857 Manchester staged a great exhibition of the arts in a crystal palace built alongside what is now the central police station. The greatest attractions of that exhibition were the concerts given in the Free Trade Hall by Mr Hallé and his orchestra.

Charles Hallé, a concert pianist, and friend of Chopin, Liszt, Berlioz, Mendelssohn and Wagner, had come to Manchester from Paris in 1848 to escape the revolution. He was in fact German, not French. His name was Carl Halle, but he anglicised his Christian name and added an acute accent to his surname so that people would pronounce it correctly.

In Manchester he gave piano lessons, travelling on the top deck of the horse-drawn trams from pupil to pupil and teaching himself English as he went along. The success of his concerts at the 1857 exhibition persuaded him to launch his own series of Hallé Concerts. The first was on 30 January 1858, and they have been going from that day to this.

And so have Mancunians. When Hallé died in 1895, the good people of Manchester formed a society to run the concerts and sent for one of the three best conductors in Europe — Hans Richter. He came from Vienna to live in Manchester, and conducted almost every Hallé Concert for the next twelve years.

The Hallé was the first professional orchestra in Britain. For over 130 years it has demonstrated that Manchester is not simply a city for merchants and manufacturers, but an arena of rich urban civilisation. In 1943 John Barbirolli became the conductor, and from the day of his arrival in the city identified himself wholly with the Orchestra. All concerts were memorable, but the incident I most enjoy recounting occurred one evening when Artur Rubinstein was the soloist. He was playing a Mozart piano concerto. He went into the cadenza and came out into the wrong concerto. Barbirolli looked at him. Rubinstein grinned, and improvised his way back into the right concerto at the right bar. And Barbirolli blew him a kiss.

After Barbirolli came James Loughran, Stanislaw Skrowaczewski, and now Kent Nagano. He endeared himself to the members of the orchestra at their first encounter. It was no secret that he had been offered many fine posts with many fine orchestras but after his first concert as a guest conductor with the Hallé, he said:

'It feels as though Manchester's time has come . . . for me.'

Manchester's time has also come for modern music. In the sixties and seventies it was Liverpool and the Mersey Beat. Since the eighties, Manchester has become the pop music centre of the world.

In the 1980s the Haçienda club played host to several up-and-coming Manchester bands − bands like The Smiths, Happy Mondays, and The Stone Roses. The Smiths may have broken up, but many of their soulful melodies and lyrics about singer Morrissey's Manchester experiences have left an imprint on the collective consciousness of the young.

The Haçienda has played host to foreign talent, in the shape of Madonna, at her first British appearance. And Manchester has also produced its own international singing superstars − Mick Hucknall of Simply Red, and Lisa Stansfield. These stars may have 'been around the world', but they have not forgotten their roots, and you are just as likely to see them out and about in Manchester as on television's *Top of the Pops* or packing the crowds in at Wembley.

With so much musical talent to hand, Manchester was the obvious choice to stage Britain's first international music convention in 1992 called 'In the City'. It was part of the annual Manchester Festival, a three-week arts jamboree which offers audiences a chance to indulge a multitude of different tastes: everything from Irish bands to Indian Kathakali; reggae to Rachmaninov.

Manchester leaves no musical tendency unrepresented.

Manchester a Celebration

Page 59: (80) Who hates Mondays? International cult band Happy Mondays led the way for Manchester to be dubbed Madchester.

81

82

(81, 82) Students of the Royal Northern College of Music serenade King Street shoppers with Christmas carols, while young musicians practise in the serene surroundings of Chetham's School in the heart of the city. (83) Charles Hallé, in contemporary caricature, founded the first professional full-time orchestra in Britain. (84) Almost within a trumpet call of the city centre, we have glorious stately homes such as Tatton Park, in the Cheshire countryside, whose grounds provide idyllic English settings for son-et-lumière events by the Hallé and other international orchestras.

83

MR. CHARLES HALLÉ.

85

86

Turn a corner in Manchester and music is in the air. Be it buskers in the city's squares and parks (85, 86, 87), or international stars in concert like Simply Red's Mick Hucknall (88, 90). Clubs such as Band on the Wall feature live music for all tastes (89).

87

88

89

90

91

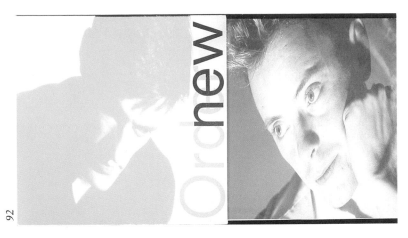

92

93

94

96

95

97

98

99

(91) Youth and style are synonymous with modern Manchester. (92, 93, 94) Album covers by bands such as K-Klass and, particularly, Peter Saville's existential leaf for New Order are statements of Manchester's youth culture. (95, 96, 97, 98, 99) The Dry Bar and the Haçienda club appear anonymous from the street but led the way to the city being accorded worldwide cult status.

100

Going home.

101

'Manchester,' wrote the Editor of *Building News* in 1861, 'is a more interesting city to walk over than London. One can scarcely walk about Manchester without coming across frequent examples of the *grand* in architecture. There has been nothing to equal it since the building of Venice.'

Cecil Stewart quoted that in the first chapter of his book *The Stones of Manchester*, which was published in 1956. An advance copy arrived at the *Guardian* office and as it made a welcome change from writing about the Suez crisis, I asked him if I could walk round the city with him.

'I would like,' I said, 'to have a close look at the best dozen buildings.'

'The five dozen, you mean,' he replied. And sure enough, on the appointed day we inspected no fewer than sixty buildings, every one of which Cecil insisted was a masterpiece. They included all the ones I had expected – Manchester Town Hall, the Free Trade Hall, the Reform Club, the Portico Library, the Bank of England building in King Street, the Refuge Assurance building in Oxford Street. But there were many more which I had walked past every day and scarcely noticed. I soon discovered that Manchester has more than its share of buildings that are aesthetic as well as functional.

Manchester's first architects were the Romans. They spent several hundred years fashioning a fort at Castlefield. But the canal and railway builders finally doused the Roman candle and buried the remains of the fort under wharfs and jetties, warehouses and viaducts.

By the thirteenth century, the city was an important trading, commercial and ecclesiastical centre and in 1421 Manchester's cathedral was built. Thomas La Warre, the 12th Lord of the Manor and rector of Manchester, had obtained a licence from Henry V to turn the existing parish church of St Mary's into a college of clergy. La Warre gave £3,000 towards the building of its replacement.

The cathedral is nothing like the original church, it has been rebuilt extensively and most of the exterior is Victorian. But inside there is still a wonderful, medieval feeling about the place, and the sixteenth century choir stalls are among the finest in Europe.

Another great survivor from the Middle Ages is the black and white timber-framed Old Wellington Inn. Having made it intact through the Civil War, Georgian and Victorian reconstruction and even the blitz, the old pub was not going to fall victim to mere postwar concrete and steel. Instead the Wellington, and Sinclair's Oyster Bar next door, were ignominiously jacked up five feet to the level of the new buildings. The antiquary John Leland visited Manchester about the time the Wellington Inn was built, and found it 'the fairest, best builded and most populous town in all Lancashire'.

It was left to the Victorians to create the city that stands today. Theirs was the cotton capital of the world, the birthplace of the Free Trade movement, and they wanted a world-class commercial city to match its international reputation. Manchester's great cotton warehouses were not just commercial buildings; they were palaces designed for the merchant princes who were the link between Lancashire cotton and its international markets.

In 1858, S & J Watts upstaged the lot with the most spectacular warehouse of them all. Each of its floors had a different architectural style – Egyptian, Italian, sixteenth century Dutch, and Elizabethan, including a glorious rendition of the Galerie des Glaces at Versailles. It cost £100,000 to build, and in 1982 £5 million more to turn it into the Britannia Hotel.

Early in the nineteenth century the cotton traders developed a new type of highly specialised structure – steel-framed packing warehouses, nine or ten floors high, and mostly clad in glazed terracotta, which now dominate the Whitworth Street area. Today, they are proving ideal to convert into new homes and offices.

Alongside all this development, Manchester's architects were frantically busy creating the corporate commercial and financial city of today. There was little attempt at homogeneity and the result is a fine diversity of architectural styles: Classical, Palazzo, above all Gothic Revival. They built the Portico Library and the Royal Manchester Institution, now the City Art Gallery (designed by Charles Barry, who went on to build the new Houses of Parliament). They built the Athenaeum and the Reform

Club, the Friends' Meeting House and the Theatre Royal, the Bank of England and the Free Trade Hall, and the Mechanics' Institute that later became the University of Manchester Institute of Science and Technology. They built a stock exchange — three in fact — to make their money and a whole battery of banks to put it in.

Alfred Waterhouse, the master of Gothic, gave Manchester many of its famous buildings — the imposing Refuge Assurance building, Owens College which became the University, and the Town Hall, to many people the finest municipal building in Britain. You could spend hours looking round the Town Hall — not least at the magnificent murals by Ford Madox Brown in the Great Hall.

When Queen Victoria unveiled Manchester's Albert Memorial, she got out of the royal train at Victoria Station to be confronted by a statue of Oliver Cromwell, for Manchester had been firmly Parliamentarian during the Civil War. Queen Victoria was not amused. Ten years later the Queen was asked to open the Town Hall.

'With pleasure,' she replied, 'if you'll take down that infernal statue.'

'Nothing doing Ma'am,' said the Lord Mayor, or words to that effect. And he opened it himself instead, to great civic pomp and ceremony.

Alfred Waterhouse was not the first architect to use the Gothic style in Manchester — nor was he the last. One of the last was Basil Champneys, who in 1899 completed the Rylands Library on Deansgate, certainly one of the most handsome, the most ornate, the most *satisfying* buildings of its kind. It has more than a touch of art nouveau and it launched Manchester with considerable grandeur into the twentieth century.

And architects have continued to serve the city well.

The Siemens building on Princess Parkway interprets the workings of the architect's pen with a rare fidelity. Crisp, clean and white, it was designed by Mills Beaumont Levy and uses modern materials and technology in exactly the way they were intended.

In contrast, the British Council headquarters makes a different statement. Designed by the Building Design Partnership, it rewards close inspection, and its central atrium is an appropriate combination of efficiency and elegance.

Ancient must live alongside modern, and in Manchester you can find some of the finest examples of modern 'infill' in the world. For example, the Civic Trust Award citation for Lincoln House on Deansgate states: 'This is a bold and joyful exercise in glass and granite, reflecting the ornate character of the buildings adjacent whilst making its own contribution as an important landmark in the city.' And that is what it is all about.

With so many listed buildings of note, Manchester has developed real skill in sensitively adapting the city's inheritance for the generations of the future.

Buildings such as Eastgate in Castlefield are a case in point. Once a thriving wharfside warehouse, Eastgate has now been given new life as a centre for the creative professions in the city. Architect Roger Stephenson has won widespread praise from his peers for this metamorphosis.

Patrick Nuttgens once said in a BBC TV programme, *Architecture for Everyman*, 'The challenge for the modern architect is the same as the challenge for all of us in our lives, to make out of the ordinary something out-of-the-ordinary.' In that Manchester has undoubtedly succeeded.

Manchester a Celebration

Page 69: (101) Among the greatest gifts of Manchester's Victorian forebears are our buildings: Manchester Town Hall is not only the democratic heart of the city but a statement of its strength.

(102, 103) In Oxford Street, the Refuge Building, started in 1894, combines soaring splendour with intricate detail. Today, part is home to the Charterhouse Hotel, while other sections are offices of distinction. (104) We treasure the nuggets of architecture like Minshull's House, first built in 1689, restored in 1890 and preserved for today's citizens.
(105) Victoriana marks the exterior of Manchester Cathedral, but within these walls are sections reaching back to the sixteenth century.

106

Grace and grandeur echo throughout the region. (106) John Ryland's Library provides a place for quiet scholarship.
(107) Lancaster House in Whitworth Street is illuminated by the morning sun.
(108) Bolton's Le Mans Crescent presents an elegant face to its citizens.
(109) Manchester's Crowne Plaza Midland Hotel is redolent with great memories like the first meeting of Rolls and Royce.

107

108

109

110

111

112

(110, 113) Within the Town Hall, civic leaders are surrounded by lasting beauty in the corridors of power. (111) Outside the Great Hall, a mosaic shows the flower of the cotton plant upon which much of our fortune was founded. (112) The symbol of the industrious bee exemplifies our past and present.

113

114

The character of the city is marked as much by new buildings as old. (114) Lincoln House won a Civic Trust award for its qualities as a modern landmark. (115) Attention to detail enhances Exchange Quay. (116) Kellogg's new European headquarters at Old Trafford indulge a love of light and spaciousness.

115

116

Gateways to a city demand buildings of
definition. (117) On the route into the city
from Manchester Airport, No 1 City
Road is a mirrored glass imprint of the
1980s. (118) Siemens enhanced their
investment in the city with their striking
headquarters building on Princess
Parkway. (119) The British Council, voice
of British culture across the world,
displays a flair for design in the entrance
to its new headquarters.

117

118

Barton Arcade is Manchester's 'little Crystal Palace', restored a decade ago as a centre for elegant shops and offices.

121

In the years immediately before the First World War, it was said that there were only two people in Manchester whom everyone recognised in the street. One, of course, was C. P. Scott, the editor of the *Manchester Guardian*; the other was Miss Horniman.

Behind her back everyone called her Queen Horniman, but no one dared say that to her face.

Annie Elizabeth Fredericka Horniman, a name which she said implicated two aunts, two grandmothers, and her father, was born in London in 1860. Her grandfather was the first man to sell tea in packets, and had made a packet. Miss Horniman spent her share of that tea money on the theatre.

Annie was a very independent young woman. She smoked; she wore bloomers and bicycled; she studied art at the Slade School. But above all she loved the theatre. She financed the first public performance of George Bernard Shaw's play *Arms and the Man*. She was the unpaid private secretary of the great Irish poet, W. B. Yeats and, at her own expense, she built the Abbey Theatre in Dublin. Then, in 1907, a letter appeared in the *Manchester Guardian* announcing that Miss Horniman planned to establish a repertory theatre in the city which would produce good new plays, revive old masterpieces, and present translations of the best works of foreign authors. Manchester had been chosen because it was a cultural centre. It supported the Hallé Orchestra and had a newspaper, the *Guardian* itself, famous for its dramatic criticism.

Haslam Mills, the *Guardian*'s famous reporter, who once cabled a semi-colon from Moscow, said that there were always two first night performances in Manchester — one in the theatre and one in the columns of the *Guardian* the following morning, when the critic 'described the adventure of his soul in the presence of the masterpiece'.

Miss Horniman came to Manchester, to the Midland Hotel which contained a proper little theatre, built because a theatre had previously stood on the site and the land had been sold only on condition that the hotel included a theatre.

The new company opened in the Midland Hotel Theatre on 23 September 1907, with a performance of a play by Charles McEvoy called *David Ballard*. The *Guardian* critic praised the adventure of his soul, and his only fear was that the audience might not be worthy of the venture. But it was. Within a few months Miss Horniman was sufficiently encouraged by the local response to buy the Gaiety Theatre in Peter Street.

In running her repertory theatre, Miss Horniman had three aims. First, that the theatre should have a permanent company (and that first company included two actors who were to marry — and achieve international fame: Lewis Casson and Sybil Thorndike). Second, that a season should rotate a number of plays in the repertoire, hence repertory. And her first full season contained more than twenty plays including works by Shaw, Galsworthy, Euripides, and Beaumont and Fletcher. Third, that new local writers should have their plays produced. And in that first season she presented plays by the local authors who were to be labelled 'The Manchester School' — Stanley Houghton, Harold Brighouse and Allan Monkhouse.

Miss Horniman ran the Gaiety until 1921, when public apathy compelled her to sell it and it became a cinema. Soon afterwards she left Manchester.

Miss Horniman's departure was not the end of repertory theatre in Manchester. Quite the opposite. It prospered both in the municipal theatres, the Library and the Forum, and in smaller ventures like the Piccolo. But I suspect that Miss Horniman herself would have been most tickled by the Royal Exchange Theatre, the theatre-in-the-round, built inside the old cotton exchange.

Theatre 69 had prospered at the University Theatre, but the University needed its theatre for its own productions and it was compelled to look for a new home. I remember I bumped into Peter Henriques, its chairman, outside the Central Library one day.

'Where,' he said, 'should we build our new theatre?'

'In the Royal Exchange,' I said.

'That's what everyone is saying,' he said, thereby dashing my claim to have thought of it first.

The response to the Royal Exchange Theatre Appeal was a clear indication that the idea of a theatre suspended in the centre of an enclosed space had caught on. The local authorities and the Arts Council were swift to see the wisdom of it, and the citizens contributed on a scale rarely seen before. They knew a good thing when they saw it, and they had seen it.

The Royal Exchange Theatre was assured of an audience because it already had a following. Everyone had his or her own favourite recollection of the days in the University Theatre. My own favourite moment was when the axe just missed Tom Courtenay in *The Playboy of the Western World*. And my favourite production was Wendy Hiller in *When We Dead Awaken*. I had gone, I recall, on a filthy foggy night; everyone was late and tetchy and in no mood for anything. And yet within seconds of the opening lines, I was captive. The production was so compelling that I could not even chatter in the interval for fear of breaking the spell. And I drove home, older, wiser, and richer in experience.

The Royal Exchange Theatre came at the very moment when Manchester was turning its attention to the reconstruction of the city centre. The city, rightly I believe, had made its post-war priorities housing, education, and social services. But now the time had come to replenish the city centre and the Royal Exchange was a good example to set planner, architect, and developer alike. Coincidentally, that new look inwards at the city was also directed to the areas around the two great existing theatres, the Opera House and the Palace. Both had their periods under threat. The Opera House became a bingo hall for a short time; the Palace nearly closed. But both were rescued. And looking back over the years I can remember great evenings in them both. Olivier as Shylock at the Opera House and the first night in Britain of *West Side Story*; Sammy Davis Jnr at the Palace and John Osborne's *Look Back in Anger*.

These days, far from closing down, the Palace hosts blockbusting West End shows. When *Les Misérables* opened in early 1992, advance bookings broke all box office records. The Opera House has a continuous programme of opera, theatre and ballet performances by leading national and international touring companies including the Glyndebourne Touring Opera, Opera North and the Welsh National Opera.

Greater Manchester now has more theatres than anywhere else outside London. The Royal Exchange continues to thrive, as does the Library Theatre, which has a mixed programme of new and traditional work. The Green Room Theatre is an exciting development in a converted railway arch in the city centre, and is one of the only houses in the country committed to contemporary work. The Contact Theatre performs the work of new, up-and-coming writers.

Many more theatres in the region have established themselves on the national network for touring companies, like the Bolton Octagon, another theatre in the round, the Oldham Coliseum and Grange Arts Centre in Oldham.

A theatre-mad friend from the south came, I recall, to spend five days in Manchester. Every night he went to a different theatre, and he was overcome.

'This place,' he said, 'is better than the West End or Broadway.'

Were he to come now he would probably add '. . . or Off Broadway', because in recent years, in addition to the commercial, municipal and repertory theatre, Manchester has also enjoyed a flourish of fringe and street theatre.

It was chosen as the City of Drama for 1994. I would argue that it always was, and always will be, the City of Drama.

Manchester
a Celebration

Page 83: (121) Victorians called the trading floor of Manchester's Royal Exchange the biggest room in the world: today it generously embraces the Royal Exchange Theatre, a unique national treasure.

122

123

124

THE · PLAY · MIRRORS · LIFE

Our zest for life is mirrored by our love of theatre, professional and amateur: we welcome groups like Oldham Youth Theatre (122) and international productions such as Les Misérables (123) to the fifteen theatres in the city (124, 125).

In the arts, as in commerce, Manchester is an international city.
(126) A long association between Manchester and St Petersburg ensured an ecstatic welcome for the Kirov Ballet at the Palace Theatre. (127) A televisual celebration, simply entitled A Simple Man, captured in dance the genius of the artist L.S. Lowry and has become a worldwide classic. (128) The Northern Ballet School is recognised for the quality of its teaching and its students.

129

Pantomime is a Christmas tradition. The much loved comic Les Dawson maintains the magic of the season by playing in Dick Whittington at the Opera House.

On 3 February 1900, in Gorton Tank School in Manchester, which had been used for the children of workers at the nearby LNER locomotive works, the first Northern Edition of the *Daily Mail* was printed.

The *Daily Mail* was the first popular daily newspaper in Britain. It was started in 1896 and its sales rapidly rose to half a million copies a day. To reach a million its owner, Alfred Harmsworth, later Lord Northcliffe, decided to print in the North as well as in London. He chose Manchester, and his enterprise was rewarded with a daily circulation of a million, and within two years the *Mail* had moved to new premises on Deansgate.

Where Northcliffe trod, others followed, but at a distance. It was 1927 when the *Daily Express* came to Manchester. The *Daily News* came a year later, in 1928, settled in Derby Street in Cheetham, and two years later changed its name to the *News Chronicle*. The *Daily Herald* arrived in Oxford Road in 1930, after a huge rally at Belle Vue. And Manchester could then claim to be the other end of Fleet Street.

But central to the whole development of the newspaper industry in Manchester was a local enterprise which began half a century earlier – in 1872 to be precise. Ned Hulton, an apprentice printer sacked by the *Guardian* for printing pirate news-sheets, decided there was a market for a daily paper devoted to sport. So he started the *Sporting Chronicle* . . . and finished up with an empire.

In 1885 Hulton launched his first proper newspaper, the *Sunday Chronicle*, and twelve years later introduced the *Evening Chronicle*, which provided lively competition for the *Manchester Evening News* for more than sixty years. And by 1900 he was ready to take on the giants: two days after the *Daily Mail* arrived in Manchester he brought out his *Daily Dispatch*, which he called the North's own national newspaper. Its circulation eventually reached half a million.

Hulton's premises in Withy Grove were to become Europe's biggest newspaper printing house. Besides the *Evening Chronicle* it printed several morning papers and national magazines, and no fewer than four Sunday papers. But none of them, it has to be said, was as good as the *Guardian*.

The *Manchester Guardian*, founded in 1821 in protest at the Peterloo Massacre, became much more than a local paper. Its circulation for many years was concentrated on Manchester, but its constituency was the liberal conscience of the land.

It was more literate, more scholarly and more influential than any other daily paper. Its editor, C. P. Scott, it was said, made righteousness readable. And who else would have sent John Masefield to cover the Easter Rising in Dublin, or Arthur Ransome to report on the Russian Revolution? (Ransome ended up marrying Trotsky's secretary.)

It gave every reporter his head (a very useful portable container, as Michael Frayn said) and it gave every commentator his freedom. To work on the Corridor, where the leader writers lived, was better than a fellowship at All Souls', and there will always be those, I among them, who wish it was still edited in the city where it was born.

Manchester's importance as a national print centre did not diminish with the *Guardian*'s removal to London. On the contrary it continues to flourish.

The *Manchester Evening News* is the country's largest provincial newspaper. It was founded in 1868, and celebrates its 125th anniversary in 1993. Like the *Guardian*, it is owned by the Scott Trust and is considered essential reading for businessmen, politicians, and other decision-makers, as well as the general public. Its five daily editions are printed in Trafford Park, along with *The Daily Telegraph*. Mirror Newspapers have opened a multi-million pound printing centre at Hollinwood, near Oldham.

Greater Manchester has no shortage of evening newspapers, with the *Bolton Evening News* and the *Oldham Evening Chronicle* and three more serving Lancashire. Liverpool has two daily papers – the *Daily Post* and the *Echo*. The combined daily readership of all these papers comes to over three million. No wonder so many of the country's best journalists come from the North West.

The success of journalism in Manchester and the North West was a great inspiration and support to those who pioneered broadcasting in Manchester, first in radio, and then in television. It gave them standards and confidence and the determination never to settle for second best. And it helps to explain why Manchester has produced so much good radio and television.

The headquarters of the BBC and ITV are based in London, but a good proportion of all their programmes are produced in the North West by BBC North and Granada, the largest station in the ITV network. BBC Manchester gave birth to *Top of the Pops*, the longest running pop show anywhere in the world, and Granada gave The Beatles, The Hollies and The Rolling Stones their first appearances on television.

Granada is the TV station responsible not only for such classics as *Brideshead Revisited* and *Sherlock Holmes* but also for the best-acted, best-written, and longest-running soap opera in the world, *Coronation Street*. And Granada's *World in Action* is a model to the emerging democracies of Eastern Europe of how to probe events.

Many of the popular BBC programmes are already recorded in Manchester, among them *A Question of Sport*, and the *Mastermind* headquarters is also moving here. The move to Manchester of the BBC's Youth Programmes department is an acknowledgement of the increasing influence of the region's youth culture. The BBC also plans to move its Religious department to Manchester, which, as I said at the time, will take them a step nearer heaven.

Action Time, the world's largest TV game show production company, has always been based in Manchester, and exports its programmes worldwide.

Manchester generated an aristocracy of broadcasting comedians, including Norman Evans, Rob Wilton, Jimmy James, Roy Castle, Jimmy Clitheroe, Ken Dodd, Al Read, Harry Worth, Jimmy Tarbuck, Morecambe and Wise, and Ken Platt. And it encouraged such writers as Robert Bolt, Stan Barstow, Alan Plater, Keith Waterhouse and Willis Hall.

Manchester is home to BBC's GMR, the biggest metropolitan radio station in the country. And one of Manchester's several commercial radio stations, Piccadilly Gold, is the largest and most successful regional independent station in the country. At the New York Radio Festival in 1992 it won a gold medal for its news coverage.

The region's influence on national and international communications can only increase, because a new generation of media talent is being encouraged by University College Salford. Founded in 1986, the Department of Performing Arts and Media Studies already has an international reputation and takes over six hundred full-time students from home and abroad. In 1991, it introduced the country's first degree in broadcasting, a three-year television and radio course, followed in 1992 with a Media and Performance course. Both have 'heavyweight' professional patrons in Jack Rosenthal the writer and Ken Russell the film director respectively. The College and the media have a close working relationship — Granada sponsors two television and radio students, and the College runs the Granada Film and Television Awards.

As a city, Manchester has an uncanny ability to identify and nurture those with something to contribute to the media. I speak from experience.

Manchester a Celebration

Page 91: (130) Sunset Radio, launched by Mike Shaft, is one of five radio stations beamed across the city's airwaves — it was the first community station providing broadcasting access for ethnic and minority groups.

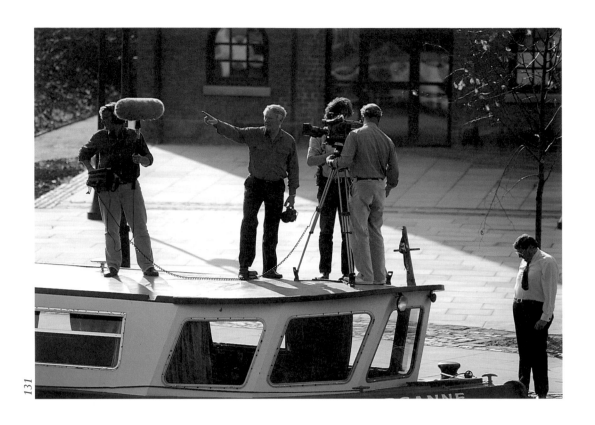

131

132

We understand how to communicate with the world. (131) The BBC has a major centre for news, sport, drama and youth programmes in Manchester. What could be more natural than a BBC outside broadcast unit filming a programme called Wish You Were Here in our welcoming city? (133, 132) We are avid readers, and great newspapers like The Daily Telegraph, the Guardian and the Manchester Evening News are printed in their millions at a computer-controlled modern plant in Trafford Park. (134) The Manchester Evening News van is a familiar sight throughout the region.

133

134

(135, 136) Humour, wit and humanity have made Coronation Street, produced by Granada Television in the city, the world's favourite and longest-running soap opera. It is broadcast in four continents.

137

A SPORTING LIFE

Everyone in the North West of England will tell you that when Liverpool manager, the late great Bill Shankly, was asked in a famous interview whether football was a matter of life and death, he replied, 'It is much more important than that.'

When I first arrived in Manchester I was no stranger to matters of life and death. Back in Newcastle I had seen Bobby Charlton play his first game for Ashington Boys against Whitley Bay Boys, and had seen Len Shackleton, in a game at St James's Park against Manchester City, run the full length of the pitch with the ball balanced on his head. In Manchester I was able to see a Manchester United that included Best, Law and Charlton, and a Manchester City which included Summerbee, Lee and Bell. Summerbee and Best were the greatest of friends. Not so the fans. One Lord Mayor of Manchester, whose allegiance was no secret, once toasted in the Town Hall 'the two great teams of Manchester – Manchester City and Manchester City Reserves'.

There were bad moments. The worst was the night of the Munich air disaster in which twenty-three people were killed, including eight members of the Manchester United team. Men stood in silent groups along Cross Street reading Tom Henry's emergency edition of the *Manchester Evening News* in stricken disbelief.

But there were, as there always are, great times. At the world famous Old Trafford Cricket Club I was lucky enough to see Washbrook's last innings and Clive Lloyd's first. And on my second son's seventh birthday I took six small boys to Old Trafford. They sat in privileged splendour in the front row of the stand and watched George Best work miracles.

The boy beside me sucked his thumb throughout the first half and never took his eyes off the ball. At half-time I asked him if he was enjoying his first First Division football match. He took his thumb out of his mouth and looked at me with eyes like saucers.

'This,' he said solemnly, 'is the best day of my life.'

It was one of the best of mine too.

It is scarcely surprising that football is an obsession in these parts. The oldest football ground in the world is in the North West – the Drill Field, home of the not so world-renowned Northwich Vics. And since 1904, Manchester has been the home of the Professional Footballers' Association, which represents over four thousand members. Even when it is time for the players to hang up their boots, it is to the same building that they can come for advice and guidance from the Footballers' Further Education and Vocational Training Society.

But it is not just football that Manchester is famous for. As a region we can truly be said to be 'sports mad' – and any sport will do!

Salford Harriers, the second oldest athletics club in the country, was the first British sports club to send a touring team to the United States – back in September 1890! The North West has the greatest number of athletics clubs in the country, with almost five thousand athletes competing every week of the year. This enthusiasm is reflected in the large number of North West athletes and medal winners in the 1992 Barcelona Olympics and Paralympic Games. And the region has high hopes for its current junior athletes, both for the 1996 Olympics in Atlanta, and – hopefully – the Manchester 2000 Olympics.

Of course, the North West now has its own Olympic Gold medallist in cyclist Chris Boardman. Who could forget the roar of the crowd as, legs pounding on the pedals of his dream-machine bike, he swept *past* his rival in the 4,000 metres Pursuit final, straight into the record books and the proud heart of every Mancunian.

There is nothing like the excitement of a good competition – and the North West has some of Britain's best facilities for putting on any number of different sporting events. The Greater Manchester Exhibition and Event Centre is a regular venue for world title boxing, while on two of its superb golf courses the region plays host to the British Open Golf Championship twice in the 1990s, at Royal Birkdale and Royal Lytham and St Anne's.

In tennis the Manchester Open, staged at the Northern Lawn Tennis Club in Didsbury each year in the build-up to Wimbledon, attracts players such as John McEnroe, Stefan Edberg, Jimmy Connors, Pete Sampras and our own Jeremy Bates.

Aintree racecourse hosts the world-famous Grand National every April – the supreme test of courage for horse and rider.

Other, less obvious, sports are well-represented. In speedway, the Belle Vue Aces of Manchester are the most famous club side in the world. Founded in 1928, the track was the only one to run throughout World War II.

Salford is the home of the English Wrestling Association, and the venue for national competitions. And the headquarters of British lacrosse is also in the region.

Any national newspaper wishing to sell well in the North West quickly comes to realise that a Northern edition, particularly of the sports pages, is essential if circulation is to increase. The *Manchester Evening News* churns out a 'Sports Results Pink' every Saturday evening, and newsagents stay open late to meet the public demand. The Pink is required reading for any true sports follower.

With so much experience of sport, and with so much enthusiasm for sport, it was no surprise that Manchester should make a bid to host the 2000 Olympic Games.

Why Manchester? people asked. And the city's Olympic Committee set out to explain that Manchester could provide everything that would be needed. Not only the facilities but the welcome. It could build the finest assembly of sports arenas, make it easy for people to get to them, and guarantee the support. But it went further. It argued that what matters is not only what a city wants and gains, but also what the Olympic Games need and get.

And what the Olympic Games need is the freedom of an open society, the support of a progressive nation, the convenience of an internationally understood language and the friendship of a people for whom sport is a universal pastime.

Manchester qualifies on all those counts.

It can offer the Olympic Games efficiency without officiousness, organisation without harassment, support without prejudice.

Manchester is uniquely placed to host the Games.

On the back of the bid, a building programme has started to provide a number of major sports facilities which will be completed irrespective of the final outcome. Win or lose, East Manchester will get a National Cycling Centre incorporating the country's first indoor velodrome and the best training facilities available – and who can complain at that?

By 1995 there will also be a 16,500 seat arena built on land adjacent to the city's Victoria Station, a facility capable of holding basketball, indoor equestrian events, ice-hockey, international opera and even pop concerts.

But sport is not the only issue here. Manchester's Olympic bid has also given rise to plans for the development of the inner city. Proposed new rail links and extensions to Metrolink to cater for the Olympic sites; government investment in urban development programmes; all this speaks of an enthusiastic and concerted effort on the part of the community to show the city at its best.

Manchester has never exactly had an inferiority complex, but its pride and passion now has an extra dimension, generated by the dual quest for sporting excellence and urban achievement. The city's name is now familiar to millions of people worldwide, simply because we have put ourselves forward as potential hosts for the greatest festival of sport on earth.

Government bodies, political parties, sporting associations, the young, the old, the participator and the fan have all had cause to unify in one common purpose. The Olympic bid process has united a city.

The Olympic bid has been good for Manchester – and Manchester would be good for the Olympic Games.

Page 97: (137) A City United in its love of sport.

138

Football is our first passion. (138) At Old Trafford the memorial clock marks the moment of the Munich air disaster. (139) A decade later, under the guiding wisdom of Sir Matt Busby, the Manchester United team that included the lavish talents of Charlton, Law and Best brought the European Cup to Manchester. (140) The most famous football stadium in the world. (141) Every club has its legions of enthusiastic fans.

139

141

140

(142) *The greatest passion in Manchester itself is reserved for the private contests between Manchester United and Manchester City. The city's footballing fame is international, with Manchester United able to claim more supporters' clubs world-wide than any other team — Pavarotti is an ardent fan (143).*

144

145

Summer turns our attention to cricket.
(144) Huge crowds throng the other Old
Trafford stadium, home of Lancashire
County Cricket Club and venue for great
Test matches. (145) On the village greens
around the region, the game is contested
with equal fervour. (146) When a match
lasts up to five days you can catch up with
the important things in life. But it is best
not to get caught out by players like Clive
Lloyd (147), former captain of the West
Indies and Lancashire, who has made his
home among us.

146

147

148

149

*Even at the top, sport is for fun.
(148) Phyllis Smith, who runs for Wigan,
relieves the tension of the 1992 Olympic
Games after winning a 4x400 Relay
bronze medal. (149) Local hero Chris
Boardman wheeled his way into
everyone's hearts by taking a Gold Medal
for cycling. (150) Exhausted but
exhilarated, Tara Flood swam into our
headlines at the Paralympics in Barcelona.*

150

(151) Support for Lacrosse is strong in our region, which has hosted that sport's World Championship in recent years.
(152, 153) Rugby League has a huge following. Fans show their own sense of humour and bonhomie for Wigan who have held the Rugby League Challenge Cup for five consecutive years from 1988.

151

152

153

154

155

(154) The countryside that surrounds us
provides a tranquil setting for scores of
superb golf courses such as Mere.
(155) The British Open championship is
staged regularly at two of our courses,
Royal Birkdale and Royal Lytham St
Anne's. (156) Skiers can practise all the
year round on dry slopes at Rossendale.

157

158

159

160

(157/158) *Windsurfing and sailing on the lovely waters of Pennington Flash.*
(159) *The pace quickens with the thrill of seeing the top names in cycling as the Kellogg's Race flashes through the city streets, and (160/161) the world's most challenging steeplechase, the Grand National at Aintree, is on our doorstep.*

161

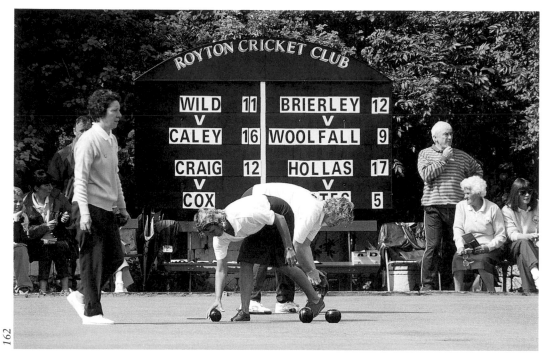

(162, 163) And when we need a more gentle pace, there is bowling; or the pleasure of angling along the banks of quiet canals and rivers.

164

The Canal Age in Britain began with the opening of the Bridgewater Canal in 1761 and reached a climax with the opening of the Manchester Ship Canal in 1894.

It was a remarkable achievement that turned an inland city thirty-five miles from the sea into the third busiest port in the UK.

The canal was born of necessity. For years Liverpool, on the coast, had Manchester by the throat, overcharging for its services – port dues and carriage rates – on everything that passed through its docks to and from Manchester.

As early as 1825, Manchester merchants submitted a plan to Parliament for a ship canal from Manchester passing through Didsbury, Lymm and Frodsham to the River Dee, which runs through Chester to the sea. Liverpool made mock of it. They used to recite a little ditty:

> Oh ye lords of the loom
> Pray avert your sad doom
> We humbly beseech on our knees.
> We do not complain
> That you drink your champagne.
> But leave us our Port, if you please.

Parliament decreed that they were to be left their Port. The merchants of Manchester continued to pay through the nose for everything that went through Liverpool. And when the railways opened, the railway companies were no less grasping. As the end of the nineteenth century approached, Manchester was in a very bad way. The cotton merchants could afford neither the exorbitant charges for bringing in the raw cotton, nor those for shipping out the finished products. Their businesses went bust, workers were paid off and the population drifted away. In 1881 there were almost twenty thousand empty houses in Manchester, and whole streets were uninhabited. No fewer than fifty great cotton warehouses stood unused, their To Let signs fading.

Then, on 27 June 1882, Daniel Adamson summoned a meeting of everyone who was anyone in and around Manchester – civic heads, merchants and manufacturers, workers' representatives and, of course, the money men and engineers. They decided at that meeting that Manchester *must* have a ship canal. There was some argument about whether it should be tidal and unencumbered by locks, or at different levels and maintained by locks. In the end, the second course was adopted.

Twice Parliament turned them down, but finally the Manchester Ship Canal Bill received the Royal Assent from Queen Victoria on 6 August 1885. There was joy in Manchester that night: cannons were fired, church bells rang out and bands paraded in the streets.

The celebrations were a trifle premature. They still had to raise the necessary £8 million to build the canal – but after several setbacks the funds were raised in the financial markets.

The first sod was cut at Eastham on 11 November 1887 by Lord Egerton of Tatton. His was the first spadeful of 82 million tons of earth that would have to be dug out. Work progressed at a rate of roughly a million cubic yards a month with a workforce of 17,000 navvies. A lot of backs to break and a lot of mouths to feed. Five railway lines were diverted to make way for the canal and 230 miles of new track laid to serve it. Along them ran 173 locomotives pulling 6,000 wagons. It was not only muscle and spade. They made good use of mechanical diggers – steam navvies, they called them. And then disaster struck. The winter of 1890/91 brought severe floods and the canal company ran out of money. Manchester Corporation had to dig deep into the public purse before it came up with a loan of £5 million.

The work was finally completed, and at half past ten on the night of 25 November 1893, the canal was filled with water. It must have been quite a sight and quite a sound. The Manchester Ship Canal opened to traffic on 1st January 1894 and seventy-one ships sailed along it that New Year's Day. Queen Victoria came in the Royal Yacht for the official opening the following May.

Not everyone cheered. Liverpool was livid. When the first two cargoes of raw cotton from the United States sailed up the canal to Manchester in that January of 1894, the shipping agents, all members of the Liverpool Cotton Association, began to offer rebates to shippers on condition that they did not use the Ship Canal. Manchester merchants soon settled that: they formed the Manchester Cotton Association and handled the shipping trade themselves.

The canal prospered and so did the Port of Manchester, whose dockers gained the reputation of being able to stow more cargo into a ship than any dockers anywhere in the world. But after almost one hundred years of profitable trading, it became evident that ocean-going ships were becoming too big to sail up the Ship Canal. At one stage there was talk of closing the Port of Manchester, which was actually in Salford, and simply filling in the docks and treating the whole area as a building site, even a housing estate.

But wiser counsels, and the vision that engendered the original canal, prevailed. In addition to continuing as a port, the site was recognised as an environmental asset, and today Salford Quays, the old Port, with its high-tech offices, its imaginative housing and retail facilities, is a delight to the inhabitants. A major programme of oxygenating water in the docks, which include a seventy six berth marina, has made Salford Quays a popular venue for

water sports and regattas as well as angling, thanks to increasing stocks of fish. The transformation has taken place, moreover, in less than a decade. Salford Quays is recognised as an important model for rejuvenation of docklands internationally. And in fact ships still regularly sail along the canal to Trafford Park, and sometimes right into Salford itself, bringing cargoes from the continent.

Today, water buses convey commuters from waterfront homes to the commercial heart of the city centre. Salford Quays is, increasingly, a tourist attraction; parties of visitors are wide-eyed as they float down the River Irwell from the Granada Studios Tour, to the hotels, bars and restaurants, both on land and afloat. Among them you are more than likely to overhear international business being conducted in a dozen languages.

Just after the Barcelona Olympics, a photographer from that stylish city came to view Manchester. For him, as for so many on their first visit, it was an eye-opener, and when he drove into Salford Quays he almost leapt from the car, disappeared for more than an hour and returned, joyfully, with a bag full of exposed film. He had discovered that not only has Salford found a new heart, but that it has been done with panache.

Oh yes, Daniel Adamson *would* have approved.

THE OPENING OF THE MANCHESTER SHIP CANAL BY THE QUEEN THE LORD MAYOR OF MANCHESTER AND THE MAYOR OF SALFORD ARE PRESENTED TO HER MAJESTY

DRAWN BY A. FORESTIER FROM SKETCHES BY OUR SPECIAL ARTIST, H. C. SEPPINGS WRIGHT

(165) In 1894 Queen Victoria opened the Manchester Ship Canal, which made Manchester the third largest port in Britain. (166) Ocean-going ships still ply the canal to serve industry along its banks. (167) Today, families live in a relaxed waterside community at Salford Quays, within walking distance of the city centre.

168

169

From strength to strength: (168, 169, 170, 171, 172) only a few years ago Manchester docks were derelict. Today the new waterfront is called Salford Quays and is lively with offices and restaurants, yet offers peaceful havens for city living.

Page 118: (173, 174, 175) The Manchester Ship Canal provides a living link from Salford Quays to the sea.

171

172

173

174

175

176

A CITY AT WORK

Manchester invented the modern world when it created the cotton manufacturing industry. Flemish craftsmen brought wool and linen weaving to the area in the fourteenth century, but it was not until cotton started to arrive two hundred years later that the real boom began. It transformed Manchester from a busy market town into a great industrial centre.

Lancashire textiles grew on the back of a remarkable quartet of eighteenth century inventions, innovations that manufacturers were quick to act upon – Kay's flying shuttle, Hargreaves's spinning jenny, Arkwright's spinning frame and Crompton's mule. Mass production replaced cottage industry and hordes of people flocked to the town to man the mills, steam-powered after 1775.

Growth was phenomenal. In 1740, cotton imports into Manchester totalled £1 million; in 1800 it was £60 million. In 1759 twenty thousand people lived in the city; by 1831 there were 142,000. And by this time Lancashire cotton accounted for half of all British exports, and Manchester was the world centre of manufacture for a hundred years.

The decline has been equally dramatic. In the 1920s there were 470 spinning companies in Oldham alone: today there are scarcely half a dozen in the whole of the UK. But the industry has survived seemingly insuperable problems. Streamlined and re-equipped, it is yet a potent force: textile and clothing companies in the North West still employ around 73,000 people, 14 per cent of the region's manufacturing workforce.

In Manchester, of course, textiles is not the only industry to recognise innovation and act on it. When great minds meet in the city, great things happen.

On 4 May 1904 at the Midland Hotel, the Hon. Charles Rolls persuaded Mr Henry Royce to give him sole rights to sell motor cars produced at the Royce works in Hulme. The prince of marketeers had met the king of perfectionists.

They say that Royce had only built one car at the time of that meeting. But Rolls clearly knew a good thing when he saw one, and within months the firm was producing the 40hp Silver Ghost which brought them fame the world over. And it was here in Manchester too that Royce designed perhaps his most famous model, the Phantom II Continental – without leaving his sickbed. I think that counts as enterprise!

Henry Ford was equally confident. He set up production of the Model T in Manchester in Britain's first factory dedicated to the production of the popular car. That was in Trafford Park, the world's first industrial estate, and for many years the largest.

Ford took on four thousand men in Trafford Park. He paid them a generous £3 a week – but they worked flat-out and were not allowed to talk. One man who yawned was sent home for two weeks to sleep it off – another was laid off for a fortnight for stroking a cat!

By 1920 Ford was producing forty-six thousand cars a year in Trafford Park, on one occasion building a Model T in nineteen minutes as a demonstration for Manchester's Chief Constable, Sir Robert Peacock, who drove off in it!

Trafford Park, of course, has many claims to fame. It was here in 1937, for instance, that Metropolitan Vickers, affectionately known as Metrovicks, developed the first working radar transmitters – and during the war twenty coastal stations fitted with their equipment made a vital contribution to Britain's air defences. After the war, Metrovicks quickly adapted radar technology for navigational use and its 'seascan' equipment, built in Trafford Park, was installed in many merchant ships, including the liners *Queen Elizabeth* and *Queen Mary*.

Wheels and wings became synonymous with Manchester. On the ground the city cornered both the luxury and popular sectors of the car market; in the air Manchester became famous for different names: the Avro Anson, the Swordfish, the Barracuda – all built in and around Manchester. And the Lancaster Bomber. A huge and graceful machine whose pilots could tell the tune of the engines by the musical resonance which hummed through the fuselage.

British Aerospace was later to continue the city's reputation for producing great flying machines with the Vulcan, the York and the Shackleton, and today produces some of the world's most successful commercial aircraft, including the ATP and the BAe 146 — I just wish the modern names were more romantic!

And British Aerospace is not just a homebird. An aircraft which by all rights should not be able to fly at all, regularly takes off from Manchester Airport carrying within its huge cargo-hold Manchester-built airplane wings for Airbus Industrie planes. The Super Guppy, as it is known, flits between France and Britain like an over-loaded bumble-bee linking Gallic and Anglo-Saxon enter-prise and helping to maintain the Manchester region's reputation as a world leader in advanced engineering.

Industry in Manchester is not just wheels and wings. It is electronics and cornflakes too!

The electronics giant, Siemens, has a headquarters in Manchester. Sir William Siemens built up his business from scratch, and at the last count it had an annual turnover of some £23 billion. The Manchester base serves five of the company's fifteen worldwide business divisions.

And the cornflakes? Trafford Park is also the headquarters of Kellogg's in Europe — and thus the home of a great British institution.

Rumour has it that real Mancunians put beer not milk on their cornflakes — the cream of Manchester as it is known. Thirty years ago there were dozens of small breweries in the Manchester area. Now only a handful remain, of which the most famous are Boddingtons and Holts (the latter still owned by the philanthropic family who also founded the Holt Radium Institute, now the renowned Christie Hospital). But it is quality, not quantity that is important. The purity of its beers is legendary — Manchester is known as the Real Ale capital of Britain.

Even I, though, must recognise that times have changed. And to survive, Manchester's approach to industrial expansion has changed as well. Walk the streets of the city today and you will still see innovation and enthusiasm — but the targets of those most creative of human elements have changed. Now the targets are jeans and records, cosmetics and advanced research. Mancu-nians were quick enough to know that to survive they must diversify — and diversify they have.

Joe Bloggs, for instance, means fashion and jeans, not anonymity and ordinariness. Multi-million pound indus-tries have been built on the audacity and determination of creative flair.

Mancunians trade in it. Factory Records, the creation of a northern entrepreneur called Anthony H. Wilson, did not overlook its found-ations. Indeed, it was the very foundations of the industrial city which helped forge Factory's fame. Wilson's Haçienda nightclub became the headquarters for a new wave of music which swept the world — and the Haçienda began its life as a warehouse helping to fuel the fire of the industrial revolution. Full circle.

Today Manchester is the financial centre of the North. The city has the best service base outside London. Its people have proved they can turn from shovel to satellite in the blink of an eye. The proof lies in the fact that the financial sector is now so powerful that businesses no longer look to London for major decisions on venture capital, corporate finance or merchant banking. The largest regional offices of the Bank of England are in Manchester. The city has attracted international banks and handles vast amounts of foreign business for national and regional customers.

In Manchester they call it flying with your feet firmly on the ground.

Manchester a Celebration

Page 119: (176) Symbols of success: modern shimmering towers mark the redevelopment of Manchester.

177

178

179

There are many milestones in

HMS BRONINGTON

A CHANCE TO SEE ONE OF THE LAST CONVENTIONAL *wooden minehunters* OF THE ROYAL NAVY - HMS BRONINGTON IS NOW BERTHED AT WHARFSIDE, TRAFFORD PARK, MANCHESTER ➤

182

183

184

(182, 184) Feed the mind and feed the man: the Co-operative Wholesale Society is one of Britain's largest employers, yet this giant of an organisation, which enabled consumers to share in the profit of stores, began with the Rochdale Pioneers in the humble surroundings of Toad Lane.
(183) Disused markets have been carefully restored to become craft and garden centres.

(185) The prosperity of the city once known as Cottonopolis is expanding as an international fashion centre with a bustling rag-trade quarter. (186) The energy of entrepreneur Shami Ahmed is known the world over through his legendary Joe Bloggs jeans and fashion empire.

185

186

187

188

189

(187, 188) Manchester is a city with an assured future. The evidence lies in a thriving Stock Exchange, and more than sixty financial institutions. (189) The Sun Alliance Insurance symbol has been a feature of Manchester's business quarter for over one hundred years.

190

126

The city has a history of investment in technology as well as bricks and mortar. *(191) Where else would the National Computing Centre be established other than in the city that developed the first commercial computer? (190) The presence of such a wealth of services is demonstrated in development at an unprecedented pace.*

(192) And even our less welcome services are delivered with a smile!

191

192

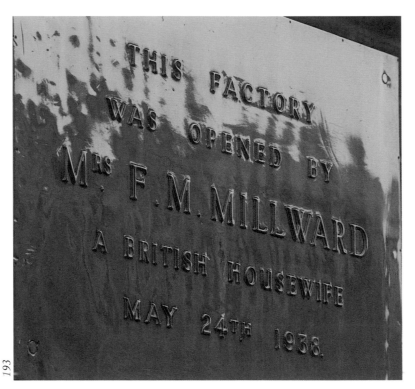

193

*(193, 196) Kellogg's asked not a dignitary
but 'A British Housewife' to open their
plant in Trafford Park.
(194, 195, 198) Throughout the region
great companies demonstrate the diversity
of wealth. (197) This explains why the
British Council located its headquarters in
the city centre.*

194

195

196

197

198

199

200

(199, 200) Brother have their European headquarters here. McVitie's make their famous biscuits in the city, and check the colour and quality every hour.

201

A glorious by-product of Manchester's importance as a centre of manufacturing and industry in the eighteenth and nineteenth centuries is the rich legacy of stately homes, mansions, magnificent country parks and opulent gardens. These were the homes of the wealthy merchants, entrepreneurs and engineers who were at the forefront of Britain's Industrial Revolution.

The splendid neo-classical mansion at Tatton Park was the family home of Francis Egerton, third Duke of Bridgewater, whose pioneering canal played such a vital role in the industrial development of eighteenth century Manchester. The house was built between 1780 and 1813, but the family history at Tatton goes much further back in time. The gardens owe their beauty to the style of landscaping popular in the seventeenth century; immaculate lawns sweep down from the front of the house to formal terraces in the Italian Garden. Giant redwoods from the Americas, exotic ferns from New Zealand, and the Japanese Garden make this one of Britain's finest estates.

Tatton Park, along with many stately homes, throws open its doors for a whole host of events: from game fairs to antique car rallies, horse trials to hot air ballooning, these houses provide the perfect backdrop. And on no occasion is the setting of Tatton put to better use than when the the Hallé Orchestra performs in front of the lake, a *son et lumière* extravaganza.

Heaton Hall, closer to the city centre, was designed by the well-known architect James Wyatt in 1772 when he was just twenty-six years old. It stands in the huge grounds of Heaton Park, the largest municipal park in Britain and the site of a host of activities enjoyed by many Mancunians. It is also home to the Papal Stone erected to commemorate the visit of Pope John Paul II in 1982, when Manchester's population came out in force to welcome His Holiness.

Hall i'th'Wood in Bolton, a striking black and white medieval merchant's house built in the fifteenth century, later became the home of Samuel Crompton. It was in Bolton in 1779 that he perfected the Spinning Mule, one of the key inventions that catapulted Britain into its Industrial Revolution.

Several other National Trust properties surround Manchester. Dunham Massey, an early eighteenth century house in formal parkland was, until 1976, home to the tenth and last Earl of Stamford. It contains outstanding collections of furniture, paintings and Huguenot silver, and in the park is an Elizabethan water mill, now a saw mill in working order.

Lyme Hall, set in a 1,300 acre wooded deer park in Disley, was home to the Legh family at the beginning of this century. The Elizabethan gritstone building dating from 1560 had various alterations and additions made to it in the eighteenth and nineteenth centuries. Today the hall houses a splendid collection of antique English clocks, tapestries, fine furnishings and paintings.

There is certainly no lack of choice for enthusiasts of fine architecture, furnishings and gardens — as a region we seem to have more than our fair share. The arresting sight of Bramall Hall is a prime example of our distinctive contribution to world architecture. Largely rebuilt in the late Elizabethan period, this charming building stands high on a knoll overlooking the park in the valley below. This was landscaped by Victorian owner Charles Nevill in the style of Capability Brown, and it gives a grand vista over the terrace, lawns and lakes to the trees beyond. In 1935 the estate was sold and was opened to public view in 1936. Today you can wander at leisure through rooms which afford a glimpse of centuries of gracious living.

Mottram New Hall, built in 1721, is a fine example of the architecture of the day, and was home to a wealthy Stockport landowner, William Wright. This listed building's magnificent ceilings in the main hall and other public rooms are classed as works of national importance. Mercifully the conversion of the hall into a hotel in 1971 was appropriately painstaking, preserving the Adam ceilings and twelfth century wood panelling taken from the original old hall which still stands as a private house in the grounds.

In 1884 Fletcher Moss, a Manchester Alderman, bought the old Parsonage in Didsbury and cherished it with unusual care. His obsessive devotion to the gardens is apparent from the beauty of the rose gardens, herbaceous borders, orchid house and rare trees and shrubs. On his death in 1919, Moss left the house and gardens to Manchester Corporation for the benefit of the local people. The city fathers very properly renamed it Fletcher Moss after their philanthropic colleague. With the gardens so close to the city centre they provide a constant source of amazement when stumbled across.

For those who prefer to delve a little deeper into the past, Gawsworth Hall near Macclesfield, along with the church and old rectory, represents a perfect picture of medieval England. Built largely in 1480, this family-owned, half-timbered Cheshire manor house remains virtually unchanged from the days of Elizabeth I, the dining room still holding a fine Elizabethan refectory table. It is here that the beautiful Mary Fitton lived. A maid of honour to Queen Elizabeth I, and reputedly the 'Dark Lady' of Shakespeare's sonnets, she was, like almost every colourful character of the day it seems, sent to the tower. Her crime? Becoming pregnant.

One of the most photographed views in the North West of England is the famous black and white Packet House at Worsley, where passengers used to alight from their journey along the Bridgewater canal. The house is mirrored in the canal water — which is a vivid orange from the iron ore that still seeps out of the forty-four miles of underground canals from the long-since closed coal mines of North Worsley. Today you can travel along this stretch of canal by narrowboat; from the Packet House you can almost sense the history you are travelling through.

The simple truth is that in and around Manchester it is perfectly easy to enjoy the history and the geography, the town and the country, the past and the present.

Page 131: (201) The Bridgewater Canal as it runs past the Packet House at Worsley.

202

203

204

How visionary were the creators of this city, that we are surrounded by parkland. (202) Graceful pillars mark the entrance to Heaton Hall, erected in 1772; today Heaton Park forms the largest municipal park in Britain. (203) Botanical gardens at Fletcher Moss are a ten minute drive from the city centre.
(204, 205) Manchester offers many exquisite parks and gardens where people may relax. (206) On an autumn walk through the grounds of Dunham Massey your nearest neighbours are likely to be a herd of deer.

205

206

207 *Daffodils herald the coming of spring at Lyme Hall.*

208

Bramall Hall's timbered frontage is a style echoed throughout Cheshire.

209

Mellow Mottram Hall is now a splendid country-house hotel with its own golf course.

210

(210, 211) History is nothing if it is not kept alive. Schoolchildren visit the kitchens of Dunham Massey to discover the experiences of yesteryear; and many wonder at the vision of the family which created the Japanese gardens. The National Trust maintains them for the enjoyment of the population at large.

211

*We nurture our treasures, of which
Tatton Park is amongst the greatest.
(212, 213) Visitors marvel at the richness
of the library and the elegance even of the
stable yard, under the guardianship of a
clock dating from the eighteenth century.
(214) The vast sweep of the manicured
gardens is, quite simply, breathtaking.*

213

212

214

215

Whether in a corner of a courtyard at Tatton Park (215) or a broader aspect at Peover Hall (216), these lovely legacies gladden the eye.

216

217

A GRAND DAY OUT

On a fine Sunday in April 1988, a large number of elderly people, most of them from Manchester or thereabouts, gathered in a quarry in Derbyshire and sang a battle song. Its chorus startled the rooks and enchanted onlookers:

> I'm a rambler,
> I'm a rambler,
> From Manchester way.
> I get all my pleasure
> The hard moorland way.
> I may be a wage slave on Monday,
> But I am a freeman on Sunday.

The singers, most of whom had long ceased to be wage slaves, and many of whom could only ramble a step or two, had gathered to celebrate the Kinder Trespass, the mass act of defiance which had begun in that same quarry on that same Sunday, fifty-six years earlier.

Not that everyone among those assembled wholly approved. Some thought the Trespass was a great irrelevance. It deflected attention, they said, from the serious business of negotiating access to the moorland country. But others, and I am one of them, think it must have concentrated minds wonderfully.

The Trespass was an important first step towards the formation of the National Parks, and today the people of Manchester have four such parks within easy reach — the Lake District, the Yorkshire Dales, Snowdonia and the Peak District which is right on their doorstep.

The North West also has more than a dozen Country Parks, with new ones opening every year. It has never been easier to enjoy the countryside without trespassing.

The development of transport links during the late nineteenth century broadened Manchester's horizons and made the resorts of Blackpool and Southport accessible and fashionable. Amid the development of hi-tech fairground attractions, Blackpool has managed to retain much of its original charm. Traditional tea-dances in the Tower Ballroom are just as much a part of life as Blackpool Pleasure Beach, a forty-two acre amusement park — and no Mancunian's upbringing would be complete without a trip to the annual Illuminations.

But it is not all seaside resorts. For those who like to get away from it all, there are beautiful stretches of more deserted coastline on the Wirral Peninsula. The Dee Estuary and Hilbre Islands are favourite haunts of birdwatchers and botanists, as is the Lune Estuary, north of Blackpool.

For steam train enthusiasts, the restored East Lancashire Railway takes passengers from Bury to Rawtenstall, crossing viaducts, passing imposing Victorian mills and the monument to Bury's most famous son, Sir Robert Peel, founder of the Metropolitan Police Force.

To the south of Manchester, Quarry Bank Mill, built in 1784 to spin and later weave cotton, tells the story of the textile revolution and the fascinating history of the mill owners, the Greg family. The mill and village of Styal, built to house Greg's workers, is one of the finest surviving examples of a complete factory colony. The entire estate is now a National Trust property.

The neighbouring cities of Liverpool and Chester are both less than an hour away. The ancient walled city of Chester, famous for its Roman ruins, quaint black and white timbered buildings and exclusive shops in the unique two-tier galleries known as the Rows, first flourished in the Middle Ages as a port, exporting cheese, candles and salt. Today, the city's economy depends on tourism, and it attracts visitors from all over the world.

Liverpool, too, has not been slow to exploit its colourful history. The converted dockland warehouses of Liverpool's historic waterfront, known as the Albert Dock, house the Merseyside Maritime Museum which connects the region's past with the rest of the world, telling the fascinating story of the emigrants who sailed from here to start new lives in America and Australia. 1992 saw the spectacular return of the Tall Ships to Albert Dock at the end of a four month race. Within the same complex is the Tate Gallery in the North, with the most important collection of contemporary art outside London. As a tourist attraction, the Albert Dock is the second most visited site in the country and it is just on the doorstep.

As well as these cities, smaller towns within striking

distance also offer us a glimpse of our heritage. Up into the hills of the Peak District, the handsome Georgian spa-town of Buxton has been recognised nationally as being of great historic and architectural significance. And south of Manchester, bordering the beautiful countryside of the Peak District and Macclesfield Forest, is Macclesfield, which has the country's only Silk Museum.

One thing that continually delights and surprises is the variety and contrast in the scenery around Manchester – there is never time to be bored. In Cheshire, the rolling plains are dotted with picturesque farms and villages. And no trip to the region would be complete without a look at the canals. The Cheshire Ring embraces sections of no fewer than six canals – each with a character all its own. My personal favourite is a beautiful stretch on the Macclesfield Canal from Marple to Bosley, and on to the folly of Mow Cop. Another man-made feature, one which dominates the Cheshire Plain, is Jodrell Bank, Manchester University's radio telescope which now has an award-winning Science Centre and Arboretum open to the public.

To the north, Lancashire offers the best-preserved industrial landscape in Britain, immortalising the days when cotton ruled the region. Then the scenery changes over again as it stretches towards Cumbria, the Lakes and the coast, leaving the historic and urban influences of Manchester behind. In the area of Lancashire known as Wyre, the landscape becomes rural, with the Forest of Bowland and small, pretty villages, acres of rich farmland and the River Wyre threading its way to the sea.

But a great day out is not confined to the outdoors alone. Manchester's many museums and art galleries offer visitors a great day *in*. The city's enthusiasm for the arts spans the past, the present and looks to the future too. Without doubt its most famous artist is L. S. Lowry.

Lowry was born in Rusholme in 1877, and moved to Salford, the scene of many of his paintings, in 1909. Fittingly, Salford Art Gallery houses the world's largest collection of Lowry's work. He studied painting for a time with Adolphe Valette, who made Lowry aware that the industrial scenes were worth painting. Valette himself moved to Manchester in 1905 and stayed for around twenty years. His depictions of Manchester's fog-bound streets record the end of an era in the city as horse drawn vehicles made way for trams and motor cars.

Manchester has numerous galleries which house many collections of national significance. They are a reminder of the city's opulence during the nineteenth century. The Pre-Raphaelites such as Rossetti, in the City Art Gallery, and the Thomas Wrigley collection of Turner, Constable and Landseer masterpieces at Bury Art Gallery, are a source of regional pride. The Whitworth Art Gallery, part of the University of Manchester, houses superb collections of textile designs and historic wallpapers.

With the wealth of history that Manchester has, it is no surprise that it boasts an abundance of award-winning museums such as the Museum of Science and Industry, UK Museum of the Year 1990, winner of the European Museum Award 1991 and winner of the English Tourist Board's Tourism for All Awards in 1992. Manchester is always keen to celebrate its past and share it with those who come after: the existence of museums covering such diverse areas as Jewish tradition, labour history, transport and the police bear witness to this consuming interest.

The simple truth is that now, as never before, Manchester offers tourists and residents alike a gateway to the region's unique history and geography. For anyone with a few hours to spare and the will to explore, it is the ideal starting point for a grand day out.

Page 141: (217) Manchester invented paid holidays for working people; today, as then, we know how to enjoy them.

218

219

221

Manchester people and visitors alike are spoiled for choice in the opportunities for quiet relaxation. (218) Half an hour's drive takes you to the Pennines, the hills that form the backbone of England. (219) You can breakfast in the city and be walking in the Lake District before lunch. (220) Stand in awe of the radio-telescope at Jodrell Bank, with a dish the size of the dome of St Paul's Cathedral. (221) Enjoy a pleasant stroll in Last Drop village near Bolton.

220

145

222

223

224

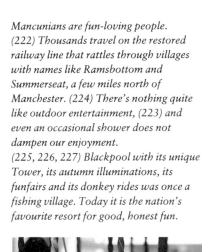

Mancunians are fun-loving people.
(222) Thousands travel on the restored
railway line that rattles through villages
with names like Ramsbottom and
Summerseat, a few miles north of
Manchester. (224) There's nothing quite
like outdoor entertainment, (223) and
even an occasional shower does not
dampen our enjoyment.
(225, 226, 227) Blackpool with its unique
Tower, its autumn illuminations, its
funfairs and its donkey rides was once a
fishing village. Today it is the nation's
favourite resort for good, honest fun.

226

227

(228) Liverpool, with its waterfront, is a world-class port of old which comes into its own with events like the Tall Ships Race. In the shadow of the Cathedral, the brilliantly restored Albert Dock bustles with stylish shops and cafés, and a museum commemorating that city's best known sons, The Beatles.

(229) Inland, at Wigan, they used to make jokes about its pier. Not any more. Today it is a major tourist centre, proudly singing of its heritage and paying particular homage to George Orwell, author of Animal Farm, Nineteen-Eighty-Four and, of course, The Road to Wigan Pier.

228

229

(231) The Museum of Science and Industry enshrines our history in award-winning style. Manchester is also justifiably proud of its twenty-three art galleries. (230, 232) The City Art Gallery hosts exhibitions of modern sculpture and displays its great collections of works like Astarte Syriaca by Dante Gabriel Rossetti. (233) The avant-garde has a special niche in the city at the Cornerhouse Gallery.

230

231

232

234

235

Peace is always close at hand in the Lake District.

236

A CITY TO CELEBRATE

Manchester is a truly cosmopolitan city. To take up residence is to belong. And people have come to Manchester from near and far.

They have brought a richness which finds expression in local culture and festivals. The celebration of the Chinese New Year and the Moss Side Afro-Caribbean Carnival are two calendar events which reflect this. It is times like these that the streets become ablaze with colour and vitality and Manchester shows the world that its musical beat is not confined to clubs and concert halls. Manchester's citizens like to be out on the street so people can hear what they have to say. The shops of Rusholme, splendidly full of spices, fruit and sweet cakes, and the agglomeration of restaurants known as 'Manchester's Curry Mile', are attractions in their own right, as are the Chinese Arts Centre and the Jewish Museum.

You may wonder why so many cultures are a part of the make-up of Manchester. For two hundred years people have been coming to Manchester to live from as far afield as China. Mostly they have come for two reasons: to escape from something or to find something, or both.

Rapid industrialisation meant the prospect of work, and for those with capital an opportunity to build business at a rate not known hitherto. But some were driven by dire circumstances to uproot themselves. The Irish community, for example, came to avoid the devastating effects of recurring famine in their homeland. In contrast, many Jewish families came to escape persecution.

People came from all over the world to settle in Manchester and many more had a profound impact on the city. Moravian refugees arrived in the 1780s to establish a settlement at Fairfield near Droylsden, an almost self-contained religious and social community whose listed Georgian houses and buildings remain to this day.

The Armenians arrived in Manchester in 1838, led by Hatzid Capamagian, and promptly built themselves a chapel. In 1870 they built themselves a church in the centre of the community in Upper Brook Street.

The Italians set up a colony in Ancoats in 1835, and by 1900 there were two thousand Italians in the Latin quarter between Oldham Street and Great Ancoats Street.

Whatever their reasons, people came to learn the new industrial skills and to settle in as merchants and manufacturers in the cotton industry for which Manchester was world famous. They brought new customs, flair and initiative which has added another dimension to Manchester's commercial growth.

The two principal communities to come to the North West in the nineteenth century were the Irish and the Jews. Even before the hungry forties, the Irish linen industry had been damaged by the success of the Lancashire cotton industry and Irish weavers came via Liverpool to weave calicoes in Wigan and muslins in Bolton. When powerlooms were invented, the English left the handloom industry and by 1835 most handloom weavers in Lancashire were Irish. The Irish also came to work on the waterfronts, in the wholesale markets, to dig canals and build roads.

The first Jews arrived in Manchester in the 1770s, tailors for the most part, with merchant outposts in Shude Hill and sweatshops in Strangeways. I remember Bill Williams, the author of the best book on the subject, *The Making of Manchester Jewry*, playing me a recording by a 97-year-old man called Philip Mosco. He had been packed off to England from Lithuania at the age of twelve, on his own, unable to speak a word of English and without friends or relatives to meet him here. But he settled in, prospered and became part of a community which was both proud of its identity and equally delighted at its acceptance.

Assimilation is too soft a word to describe the Jewish contribution to Manchester. It is more accurate to say that it was, and is, part of the richness of the city, a great addition to its character and to its prosperity, as the Manchester Jewish Museum testifies.

Most of the immigration into Manchester in the first half of this century was political and European; Jews fleeing from the oppression of Nazi Germany, Ukrainians fleeing from the oppression of the Soviet Union. But since 1950 Manchester, like most European gateway cities, has witnessed Commonwealth immigration, the migration of people from Britain's former Empire. One estimate, I recall, calculated that there were about ten thousand people belonging to the Indian community, ten thousand Pakistani and Bangladeshi, and almost twenty thousand West Indians in the city in the mid-eighties. But that was a count of those who had come from abroad and not of the second generation who had been born in Manchester. They, it is rightly argued, are Mancunians.

And that, I think, helps to explain why Manchester is genuinely a cosmopolitan city in the real sense of the word. It is accustomed to embracing incomers. And it does not look upon the arrival of people with differing creeds or differing languages as a problem, but rather as an opportunity. There may be difficulties but they can be overcome. I remember an elderly West Indian, interviewed in Moss Side, saying solemnly to a *Manchester Evening News* reporter: 'Manchester is a city, united . . . except when it comes to football'.

Diversity enriches the city, as Manchester's China-town demonstrates. Manchester has the fastest growing Chinese population in Europe, and its Chinatown is the centre of business and commerce for the estimated twenty thousand members of the community. Their enterprise has not only transformed the appearance of the area their businesses occupy, it has transformed the area's fortunes.

It is this wonderful multicultural aspect which breathes much of the life into Manchester's streets – and it is in the streets that many of the great multicultural events take place. In 1992 there was the glorious and hugely successful European Markets Festival, where traders from eleven countries gathered in Manchester, making it possible to shop around Europe in a day. The annual Lord Mayor's Parade is a similarly colourful affair, which also took Europe as its theme in 1992.

To live in the city is to understand that it is not merely a harmonious collage of *separate* communities: it is *one* multi-racial community, united in its opinion that Manchester is home.

Page 153: (236) We welcome the world to Manchester and know how to share the pleasure of each other's cultures.

Stroll through the city and you capture the universal essence of our people.
(237) With the largest Chinese population in Europe, Manchester has been accorded the status of a Dragon City. The grand Imperial Arch, around which the annual Chinese New Year festival erupts in sound and colour, is at the heart of Chinatown, whose restaurants are acclaimed in international food guides.

(238, 240, 241) *In Manchester, you are among friends. Whatever your age you can fulfil your choice of simple pleasures in a city which constantly surprises.*
(239) *Time to reflect on what might have been.*

242

243

(242) *Rusholme's Curry Mile has the best Asian restaurants in Britain and draws visitors from far and wide;*
(243) *but the lunchtime butty is also alive and well!* (244) *Sometimes though, our love of good food becomes even more obvious!*

(245, 246) *Ours is a gentle, friendly humour. We love to laugh with our guests and to laugh at ourselves, whether greeting Pope John Paul II at Heaton Park or blowing our own trumpet at the Castlefield Carnival. (247) And our zest for life proclaims our great ambitions to share our city with the world.*

248

(248, 249) *Where would you find a giant inflatable Santa Claus perched on the top of the city's seat of power, the great Victorian Town Hall? In Manchester, of course, where the Lord Mayor makes a vivid entrance at the annual civic parade. This is a city in touch with its people.*

249

250

251

252

(250, 251) Morris men, adorned with ribbons and bells, perform their traditional dance outside a city pub.
(252) Whole villages turn out in costume for the Rush-bearing Festival that has been maintained down the ages in Saddleworth.
(253, 254) Costume from a farther world and the timeless fun of a child's painted face bring gaiety to Moss Side carnival.

253

254

255

256

Simply hanging around (255) and puzzling over street theatre (256) are part of childhood.

2.57

A FINAL WORD

We look back now on the Manchester of a hundred years ago, when the Ship Canal opened, and we say, quite correctly, that what was achieved then transformed the place.

A hundred years from now, I believe people will look back on what is happening in Manchester today and pass a similar judgement. Indeed they may go further. They may well say that in the last years of the twentieth century Manchester revered its past as never before, enjoyed its present as seldom before and prepared for its future as rarely before.

Not very long ago, in spite of all the post-war achievements in Manchester and the North West, there was hesitation and doubt. Not now. Today there is a confidence that is the true character of Manchester. It is there wherever you turn. People are finding new uses for old buildings, adding others, planning more. The centre of Manchester is being sensibly redeveloped in every direction. Something new is happening at every road junction.

A hundred years ago the people of Manchester were confident that they could make a better job of things than anybody anywhere else in Britain. And that is true again. Ask anyone in a Manchester street which is the second city in England, and they will tell you: 'It is a choice between Birmingham and London.'

Implicit in the answer is that Manchester is the first city in the land.

Page 165: Sunset over the city.

Towering strength: the heart of a city at peace with itself.

258